© Jeremy Kelly

The Boy with Big Decisions is Helen's seventh novel. She lives just outside Sheffield and has worked as an actress for many years. She now prefers writing the stories rather than starring in them and can be found tapping away in her writing room with her whippet, Billy, for company.

@HelenRutterUK
www.helenrutter.com

Also by Helen Rutter

The Boy Who Made Everyone Laugh
The Funniest Boy in the World
The Boy Whose Wishes Came True
The Piano at the Station
Reggie Houser Has the Power
Me and My Brian

THE BOY WITH BIG DECISIONS

HELEN RUTTER

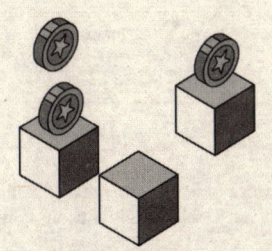

■ SCHOLASTIC

Published in the UK, 2025
Scholastic, Bosworth Avenue, Warwick, CV34 6XZ
Scholastic Ireland, 89E Lagan Road, Dublin Industrial
Estate, Glasnevin, Dublin, D11 HP5F

SCHOLASTIC and associated logos are trademarks and/or
registered trademarks of Scholastic Inc.

Text © Helen Rutter, 2025
Cover illustration by Shaivalini Kumar © Scholastic, 2025

The right of Helen Rutter to be identified as the author of this work has
been asserted by her under the Copyright, Designs and Patents Act 1988.

ISBN 978 07023 1466 7

A CIP catalogue record for this book is available from the British Library.

All rights reserved.
This book is sold subject to the condition that it shall not, by way of trade or
otherwise, be lent, hired out or otherwise circulated in any form of binding
or cover other than that in which it is published. No part of this publication
may be reproduced, stored in a retrieval system, or transmitted in any form
or by any other means (electronic, mechanical, photocopying, recording or
otherwise) or used to train any artificial intelligence technologies without
prior written permission of Scholastic Limited.

Printed in the UK
Paper made from wood grown in sustainable
forests and other controlled sources.

5 7 9 10 8 6 4

This is a work of fiction. Any resemblance to actual
people, events or locales is entirely coincidental.

www.scholastic.co.uk

*For (Dame) Amy Jeffrey –
you are a wonder*

CONTENTS

The Parents	1
The Schools	9
The Bus-Stop Decision	17
The Gains School	23
The Pressure	29
The Team Decision	35
Browtree	41
Agree or Disagree	49
The Where-to-Sit Decision	55
Rupert's House	59
The Basketball Team	67
The Bullying Decision	73
The Art Room	81
The Lies	89
The Anger Decision	95
Sit with the Naughty Kid	103

Jared	109
The Fire Decision	115
Next to Marco	123
Maisie Marvel	129
The Secret	135
Stand Up to the Bullies	141
Everything Forgotten	147
The Fight	155
The Bald Lady	163
Drawing the Poster	169
The Consequences	175
Graffiti	185
Rupert Comes Home	191
Telling the Truth	199
Trashing the Room	207
Mr Sourden	211
Mum and Dad	219
Running Away	227
The Long Walk Home	233
The Police	239
The Rescue	249
Mrs Rumbelow	253
The Gains	259
Lying to Madeleine	267
The Mystery of Marco	275

The Hospital	283
Telling Marco's Secret	289
The Office	295
Owning Up	301
One Month Later (Story Ending 1)	307
One Month Later (Story Ending 2)	311
One Month Later (Story Ending 3)	315
One Month Later (Story Ending 4)	319
One Month Later (Story Ending 5)	323
One Month Later (Story Ending 6)	327
One Month Later (Story Ending 7)	331
One Month Later (Story Ending 8)	335
The Decision Map	338
Acknowledgements	340

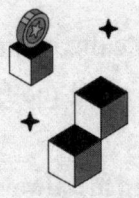

THE PARENTS

My parents don't like being called Mum and Dad. I call them by their names. Madeleine and John. People think it's weird. I saw a woman's face scrunch up in the supermarket when she heard me asking Madeleine what we were having for tea, so I try not to call them anything any more. It's harder than you think, not using people's names. I can't exactly say "Oi, you over there, what we having for tea?" can I?

People think I'm quiet or shy when I'm out and about, but I reckon if I could just say Mum and Dad like a normal kid I would be chattier. I've never asked if I can do it. Maybe they would let me, but I don't want to upset them. Madeleine is stressed all the time anyway, and John would just go on at me about it if I asked. I kind of see their point. Mum and Dad are what everyone is called, and they don't call me "child" or "boy", they call me Fred, so why not use their names too?

Madeleine and John are always very sure of things. Of what's right and wrong, of what they want and what they don't want. I'm not so clear. This morning I got stuck deciding which pants to wear for about ten minutes. The soft ones with the hole in or the new, scratchy ones that Madeleine bought me. It felt like I was frozen. It's happening more and more recently. The feeling where I can't decide, the flip-flopping, rising panic between two choices. It doesn't even have to be an important choice to make me freak out. What glass to put some squash in can send me into a spin. I can spend twenty minutes deciding which coat to put on. Luckily I don't have to make that many decisions.

My parents always tell me what to do. They decide what video games I can play, they tell me exactly when I need to do my homework, even if I'm totally not in the mood, they make me play sports that I don't like, they decide what I should eat when we go to a restaurant.

"Fred, don't get the fish and chips – you always get chips. Have the risotto."

I don't even argue any more. It's weirdly helpful.

It means I don't worry about doing the wrong thing. Making the wrong choice. They have a schedule for literally everything. Chores, meals, TV, free time. Everything is decided and written into a chart and stuck on the magnetic board in the kitchen. I just do what the chart tells me to.

I let them put out the cereal they think I should eat in the morning, choose what clothes I wear, and I let them watch me getting destroyed on the rugby pitch every single week, when surely they can see that I'm terrible.

Last time I was forced to play, before we moved here, I was standing on the edge of the rugby field as usual, hoping to get away with not getting involved. I was seeing if I could cross all my fingers over one another on both hands at the same time when – *thud* – someone barged into me and knocked me flying. Just when I thought it was over, someone else landed on top of me. I ended up with a black eye and a sore shoulder – it was awful. I thought that it might make Madeleine and John realize that rugby is not for me, but no chance. They looked all proud and said that it would toughen me up. I don't want "toughening up", though. I don't want to play rugby or hockey or any team sports. John says being part of a team is important, but not for me. All I want to do is draw and you don't need a team for that.

My parents think that drawing is pointless. They call my drawings "strange" and put them out with the recycling if I leave them on the table. So to keep them safe, I hide my pictures of imaginary machines and robotic creatures behind the boring art that Madeleine has hung on my new bedroom wall.

We've just moved house and she decorated my room. She chose the dull beige colour and sea-life duvet cover and then she hung boring paintings of boats on the walls. She thought I would like it because I love the sea, but the pictures are bad and the octopus duvet is babyish. I didn't tell her, though, because she'd already done it all. Made all the decisions for me. I just nodded, said thank you and then flipped the duvet the other way.

When I was lying on my new bed, trying to think about how I would have decorated the room, if I'd been given the choice, I didn't know. Maybe they've made so many decisions for me that I'm forgetting how to make them for myself. I looked at the pictures and tried to think about what I would like to look at. Then I realized I would like to have my own art on the walls. But I know Madeleine would find a way to take them down, say they look "messy" or just not tell me and throw them away. That's when I took a boat off the wall and secretly taped one of my pictures to the back of it. When it was back up on the wall it felt good knowing that one of my drawings was hiding behind it. That's how it feels, as though I'm like one of my secret drawings hiding behind my parents, when they answer a question on my behalf or tell me what I should do or who I am.

I'm just taping my latest artwork to the back of a boat, staring at the pencil lines. I'm really proud of it. It's of loads of sets of concrete steps leading to different-coloured doors. Some of the doors are old and have hundreds of padlocks on, and some are shiny, bright and modern. The stairs all go in different directions and link together, making it hard to get to the perfect door. My pictures are a bit like dreams. I'm not sure where they come from.

"Fred, come on. We're going in five minutes," Madeleine's voice calls up the stairs.

We're going to look around schools this afternoon. There are two secondary schools near enough to the new house. Madeleine and John have pretty much already decided. They want me to go to the Gains School because that's where John went. He thinks it's perfect and didn't even want to look around Browtree High but Madeleine said that we should "look at all the options".

I don't see much point in me going with them, as they will just tell me what to do anyway. I can't believe I'm starting secondary school in a whole new place. I wish I could have gone to King Edward's with Tommy and Frazer like I was meant to. I wouldn't mind sitting on a bus for an hour every morning, but when I suggested it to John, he snorted and told me to stop being ridiculous.

They didn't tell me that we were moving house until the first week of the summer holidays. They said it had happened really quickly and they didn't want to worry me. It was more worrying having to pack everything up super quick and tell Tommy and Frazer that we couldn't do all the things we had planned for the summer because I wouldn't be there. Madeleine and John just kept saying how exciting it was and how perfect the house was.

The only exciting thing about it is that I can walk to the beach. We have been here for two weeks now and I've been to the beach every single day. I don't go to the bits where all the squealing kids and people having barbecues and drinking beer go, because

I have found a spot. My very own spot that no one else knows about. You have to climb and scramble up some rocks, and it only exists when the tide is out, but it's perfect. A tiny circle of sand just big enough for my bum, sheltered by rocks so no one can see me. The sea lapping or crashing as far as I can see. Sometimes I take my sketch pad and sometimes I just sit. It's the only place that I feel like myself. A place where I know who I am and what I want, without the rest of the world telling me what to do.

"Fred, come on!" Madeleine calls again.

Right, I'd better go and look at the school I'm being sent to.

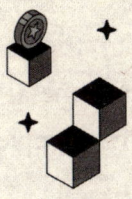

THE SCHOOLS

The Gains School is huge. It has massive iron gates and signs everywhere saying how old it is. When we go in, there are wooden plaques on the wall with lists of names and John gets all excited thinking he might spot his name.

I think it feels like something from a horror film and my face obviously looks weirded out because Madeleine holds my hand and says, "It's strange it being empty, isn't it? It would feel very different full of kids and laughter."

She's trying to make me feel better but the idea of children laughing in these empty halls just makes it feel even more ghostly. I'm taking it all in so that I can draw it later. I'm imagining a huge, mechanical squid breaking through the floor and suckering all the ghost children on its metal tentacles.

"Hello, Mr and Mrs Timple. And you must be Fred? I'm Mr Sourden."

I'm dragged out of my draw dream – that's what I call it when I think of a new picture, like a daydream but of a drawing – and see the head teacher standing in front of me holding out his hand for me to shake. He's so tall that I feel like I might fall over when I look up at him. When I feel John nudging me, I remember to put my hand out and shake the long arm of Mr Sourden.

"Thank you so much for letting us look around in the holidays," Madeleine says, smiling.

"No problem at all. I'm here anyway, preparing for next week when it all starts again for another year. Shall I show you around?"

As he glides along the corridors and leads us into room after room, I follow and feel completely lost. There's no way I will remember my way around this place. John is laughing and asking about old teachers and remembering science labs and history rooms. He seems so happy here, at home. I can't ever imagine feeling like that in this strange, echoey place.

When we leave, Mr Sourden says that he hopes to

see me next week and I smile and nod as if I agree, but inside I'm praying that I never have to set foot inside the school ever again.

"Well, the results are amazing," John is saying as he drives us towards Browtree High. "The facilities are even better than when I was there. The sports teams are at the top of every league and it sounds like the head is doing a fantastic job."

As I listen to him speaking, I know that it's a done deal. He has made his mind up. I risk a question from the back seat.

"Is there any point in going to Browtree?" I ask.

Madeleine turns and smiles at me. "I've booked it in with the head teacher so it's only polite, and you never know, we might be nicely surprised."

I smile and stare out of the window. I know that John won't change his mind. Once he's decided on something, that's it. I can just see the sea peeking through the gaps in the buildings as we whizz past, and I try and breathe it in, getting used to the fact that I'm going to the Gains School and there is nothing I can do about it.

Browtree High looks tiny. It's a series of low, modern buildings all linked by external covered corridors. Some of the buildings look like they have only just been built and some are older and uglier. It feels like one of my drawings again but this time like a spider-plant building growing extra baby buildings. When we see a woman waving at us from the door in the centre we instinctively wave back and head her way.

"She seems a bit too casual to be the head teacher," John mutters as we get nearer. "What's her name again?"

"Mrs Petts," Madeleine says.

"She's wearing jeans," John says a bit too loudly.

Mrs Petts smiles and tells us to follow her. She walks with a limp and has frizzy hair and reminds me of one of my old teachers at primary school.

"So, is there anything that you really want to see, Fred? What do you enjoy doing?"

I immediately think of art, but John answers for me.

"We would like to see everything, of course, but Fred is very sporty so maybe we could start in the sports hall?"

I sigh and follow them into one of the outside corridors and then through another door into a hall.

"We're not a big school and so we don't have the same space as some other secondaries but I like to think we're small but perfectly formed."

John glances into the hall and raises his eyebrows. Not impressed.

"Shall I take you to the science labs, or we could go to the art block next door?" Mrs Petts asks, looking directly at me. It's as though she knows. Knows not to ask my parents but to look at me and try and figure out who I am. When she says "art", I smile and nod quickly, and she winks and leads us out of the hall.

As we walk out into an external corridor, I look up and the roof is covered in graffiti. Swirling, colourful bubble letters and images filling the space. I stop and stare.

"Pretty cool, huh? Our GCSE art students did it last year. This year it will be designed by the new Year Elevens. If you came here, maybe you would like to be involved."

I smile and she carries on into the art block. Every inch of wall is covered in paintings, murals and sculptures. I don't know where to look.

"We are very lucky when it comes to art. Our teachers are the best and the facilities are very unique. Do you like art, Fred?"

Before I can answer, Madeleine says, "He's constantly doodling." Mrs Petts smiles politely.

"Not really a job, though, is it, art?" John says.

Mrs Petts looks at him and whispers, "I won't tell the art teachers you said that!" And she then gives me another wink.

After seeing the lunch hall and the science labs, John says that we have to go. I can tell that Madeleine thinks he's being rude so she says thank you too many times.

"Well, I will hopefully see you next term, Fred," says Mrs Petts.

She looks back to my parents. "Sadly, I won't be here for the first couple of weeks of term." She taps her knee. "I'm booked in for surgery. Terrible timing really but needs must. Our fabulous deputy, Mrs Rumbelow, will be running the show while I'm away. Just let me know your decision in the next few days."

As we walk silently back to the car, John says, "I will let the Gains know today and then we can get your uniform sorted in time."

I look back towards Browtree and Mrs Petts waves again. I wave back and feel my belly do a little flip and my face get tight. It feels as though I'm losing something that I never even had in the first place. For the first time in a long time, I know exactly what I want. I also know that I can't have it.

"You OK, Fred?" Madeleine asks.

Now is my chance. The time to say something. To make a decision. To tell them what I want. I try and find the words, but as I look at their faces, so clear, so sure of what's right for me, I feel the rising panic of not knowing what to do. Of not being sure enough of what to say. So unsure that I can't say anything. I give up and nod. John smiles.

"Great, off to the Gains it is."

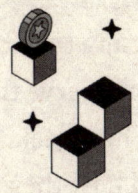

THE BUS-STOP DECISION

I nearly manage to say something to Madeleine when we're out shopping for stationery a few days before school starts. I think she's the one to talk to, as I don't think she's quite as obsessed with the Gains School as John is.

"Are you excited, sweetie?" she asks, as we leave WHSmith with a new scientific calculator and pencil case.

"Kind of," I say, knowing that it's probably my last chance. "Did you hate Browtree?" I mumble.

"No, I didn't hate it." Then she pauses, choosing her words. "It just felt a bit … relaxed."

I think about this for a moment.

"Is relaxed bad?" I ask.

"No, not at all, I'm sure that for some kids it works perfectly fine, but you deserve the best."

I bite the inside of my cheek.

I don't understand how they are so clear on what "the best" is. Could it be that "the best" is totally different from one person to the next? If so, what is my "best"? It doesn't feel like it's the Gains, that's for sure. I risk one more question.

"Didn't you find the Gains a bit scary?"

Surely she can see? Surely she can understand that I don't want to go there? Surely I don't need to say anything else? She looks at me and I think that she's got it and that she is about to hug me and tell me it's OK and that I can go wherever I want, but she shrugs and smiles.

"It'll be fine once you get there. Shall we pop to Clarks next and get you a nice pair of smart shoes before picking up your new uniform?"

I nearly say something else. Try and make it even more obvious that I don't want this, but as I search for the words, I get stuck on what to say. Maybe they are right. Maybe the Gains School is the best. As I struggle with my thoughts, she heads off in the direction of the shoe shop and I've missed my chance.

*

On the first day of term I'm standing by the kitchen door in my new uniform. The tie is annoying and won't go flat, the trousers are itchy and the green blazer is about five sizes too big. I think about the Browtree uniform. A red jumper with their emblem, a huge oak tree, printed large on the back. It actually looks pretty cool. I imagine myself wearing that instead. As it is I'm dressed up like a right nugget and itching from head to toe.

I have to be at the bus stop for 8.05 a.m. John has already gone to work. He wakes up at six o'clock every morning and leaves the house with his packed lunch at exactly six forty-five. He works in an office doing something called IT solutions, whatever that is. Something to do with computers. Madeleine works in a doctor's surgery for two days and spends the rest of the week cleaning and re-cleaning the house. She hoovers the carpet, telling me to lift up my dirty feet even when all I have on is a fresh pair of socks and the carpet already looks pristine.

The new house is completely beige. Beige sofa, beige walls, beige carpet. Beige makes me feel sick. Frazer from my last school had five brothers and sisters and they all got to choose what colour to paint their bedrooms. Every room was bright pink or turquoise or rainbow striped. I couldn't believe it. Even the downstairs was bright too, with an emerald sofa and yellow walls. It was so messy and loud and colourful, the complete opposite to our house. Sometimes I feel like maybe I was born into the wrong family or maybe I was swapped at birth or something. Maybe there is a kid somewhere who loves clean beige houses and is trapped inside colourful chaos and we should just swap.

I say bye to Madeleine and she waves me off from the front door. On the way to the bus stop I tap my pocket and check that I've got the bus fare. Then I think that I may have forgotten to pack my sketchbook so I check the time and sling my bag on the bench by the post box. I've got time to quickly check before the bus. I need my sketchbook, especially on day one. If no one talks to me I can just hide somewhere and draw my mechanical-squid version of the Gains School.

As I'm unzipping the bag, something catches my eye. Next to the bench, peeking out from under a bush, is a flash of red fabric. It feels familiar and I look around to see if anyone is watching. When no one appears, I bend over, take the red material and pull it out from underneath the bush. A huge oak tree unfolds and I see the words *Browtree High* embroidered on the front in blue thread. I check again to see if anyone is watching. It feels strange, like the wind has stopped for a second. Like this is some kind of sign. I grab the jumper and run with it in my arms to the bus stop.

I don't know why I'm holding on to it. Why I didn't leave it on the bench for the owner to find. But here I am, all alone at the bus stop, with a Browtree jumper in my arms. At five past, a bus pulls into the stop with the words *The Gains School* across the front, and as I'm about to climb aboard I see another bus pulling in behind it. Different words are written across the front: *Browtree High*.

I look at both buses and then at the jumper in my arms. An idea lands in my brain and makes my eyes open wider. I couldn't, could I? I feel the familiar feeling of flip-flopping, rising panic. Of a decision needing to be made. Which bus should I get on? Should I listen to my parents? Or is the jumper in my arms a sign? A sign that I need to do something different for a change? My eyes dart between the buses. As the doors open for the Gains School, I feel sick at the idea of stepping on to the bus, of doing the thing that my parents want me to do, that doesn't feel like the thing I want at all. I look to the Browtree bus and see kids sitting at the top in their red jumpers. I could just put the jumper on and become one of them. They look so happy, but I couldn't get away with it, could I? I can't just go to the wrong school. There's no point even trying. My head is swimming.

"You getting on, son?" the voice of the driver calls out to me, as I stand frozen on the pavement. I just can't decide. I need help. What would you do?

If you think I should **get on the Gains bus**, turn to **page 23**.

If you think I should **put the jumper on and get on the Browtree bus**, turn to **page 41**.

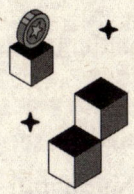

THE GAINS SCHOOL

The driver says again, "Are you getting on or what?"

This time he sounds angry. I quickly dump the red jumper in the bus shelter and step on to the bus. As I take my seat, I turn my head and stare out of the back window, watching the Browtree bus get smaller and smaller until we turn a corner and it vanishes.

I shake my head and smile to myself. I can't believe I even considered getting on the wrong bus! It would never have worked. They would have found out straight away that I was at the wrong school and called my parents. I would have been in so much trouble. But a tiny voice in my head tells me that it would have been worth it. At least then my parents would know how I feel, without me having to say it to them. Oh well – I'm on my way to the Gains

School. Living out the decisions that they make for me, as usual.

I look around the bus and see some other kids who must be new as well; their blazers look as ridiculously big as mine. At the back are kids with braces and spots, who look far too big for their bodies. They must be much older. Everyone's heads are down, vacant faces lit up by phones. You can stare at anyone when they're on their phone and they never notice. It's like the outside world vanishes. I spend ten minutes staring at people without them knowing and then when I'm bored, I get my sketchbook out.

I draw a bus that is being ripped in two with another bus coming out of it. It's pretty cool but I don't have time to really get going as the bus stops and people start getting up. We're here. I close my sketchbook and take a deep breath in. Out of the window I can see the huge iron gates and children piling through them towards the terrifying school building. I'm almost surprised there's no mechanical squid emerging from it.

"First I couldn't get you on the bus, now you won't get off! Come on, lad, wake up." It's the grumpy voice of the bus driver.

"Sorry," I call, as I shove my sketchbook in my bag

and jump up from my seat. I had no idea the bus had emptied. On my way to the doors I drop my pencil and it rolls under a seat. As I'm fumbling around for it the driver shouts, "GET OFF THE RUDDY BUS!"

So I have to abandon my pencil, even though it's one of my favourites. I scramble off the bus and look back at the driver, shaking his head and closing the doors behind me.

Part of me wishes that I'd made the other choice and got on the Browtree bus. I bet the driver of that bus was less angry. Maybe he was even friendly and fun and played music the whole way. I'll never know.

I turn to the school and hear a bell ring. The kids all start walking faster into the grey building. I catch up and follow them in. Madeleine said that all the Year Sevens have to go to the hall first to be put in their classes. I have no idea where the hall is. I can't remember how to get anywhere in this huge building with its identical classrooms and long corridors. I'm standing in the entrance and I can go either way. Left or right. I feel the familiar feeling of not knowing, but before it can turn into full-blown frozen panic, I spot a boy who is half my size and whose sleeves look like they're dangling way beyond his hands. He must be a Year Seven. He turns right so I follow him.

As the older kids funnel off to various classrooms, the corridor is left with new kids. Ahead of us we can see the head teacher's face and shoulders towering over the tiny kids. He's standing by a huge set of double doors that lead into a grand-looking assembly hall. He nods as kids walk in and occasionally stops them to adjust their tie or tell them to tuck their shirt in. At least I have found the hall! It already feels like the longest morning of my life. If the rest of the day is like this, I'll be exhausted.

I keep following the boy with the long sleeves and sit in a chair next to him. The hall fills up and whenever anyone talks there's a violent shushing that comes from the back of the room. I try to see which teacher can make a *shush* sound so intense, but every time it happens I turn round and it stops. Like a game of Grandma's footsteps but with angry shushing instead. It makes me think of a drawing of a robot with its finger to its metal lips, but before I can go fully into my draw dream, Mr Sourden glides on to the stage.

"Knowledge itself is power. *Ipsa scientia potestas est.*"

He pauses dramatically, as if he thinks we will all spontaneously applaud. When we don't, he carries on.

"This is the Gains School. Here, we expect you to be the best. Nothing will go unnoticed. An untied shoe or an odd sock, a forgotten pencil or a tapping foot. That is where the rot sets in. We will have no rot in the Gains School. If you work hard, listen and learn, then you will leave the Gains School a better version of the person you are today."

It all sounds a bit intense to me. He carries on talking for about twenty minutes about all the ways we can get a detention and then sends us in alphabetical order to line up and get instructions for where to go. By the time the T's are told to stand up, I've nearly drifted off to sleep, which was definitely on the list of ways to get into trouble. The long-sleeved boy gets up at the same time and we head towards the teachers handing out pieces of paper. I peek at the girl in front's piece of paper, which tells her that her class name is **EXCELLENCE** and where she needs to go to become a better version of herself.

"Timple?" calls a lady with tiny glasses. I put my hand up and she hands me a piece of paper. It reads:

YOU ARE IN CLASS:
<u>**DECISIVE**</u>
Please make your way to room SC12.

As I walk out, looking at the paper, I immediately need to make a decision about which way to go. The word **DECISIVE** seems to grow on the page, making the worry in my chest grow with it.

The boy with the long sleeves comes and stands next to me and shows me his paper.

"We're in the same class," he says. "I'm Rupert."

He pulls up his gigantic sleeve and holds out his hand for me to shake.

"I'm Fred," I say, shaking his tiny hand. "Do you know where you're going?"

"Yup, follow me."

As the words leave his mouth, a violent *shush* comes from the hall and this time it's close and directed right at us. The power of it makes me jump and I look in the direction it came from. A terrifying woman with a bald head has her finger on her lips and is scowling at us. Rupert starts walking and I follow. This place is worse than I thought, but at least Rupert seems to know where he's going.

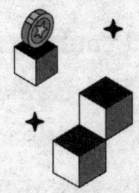

THE PRESSURE

When I get home, I'm completely exhausted. I spent the whole day following Rupert from lesson to lesson and gathering more and more books and information from various angry teachers. By the end of the day, my bag was heavy and my brain was full. The only lesson that looks vaguely interesting is DT. We're going to make a night light and can do any design we like. I'm going to make an octopus out of acrylic. Other than that, it was all English and maths and science. Thursday, I have art in the afternoon so that's my best day of the week.

When I walk through the door, Madeleine is behind it with the hoover and we nearly crash into each other.

"Be careful, Fred!" she shrieks, as though the world is about to end. "Honestly!"

I'm not sure how I could be more careful about opening the front door. How was I to know she was crouching behind it with a hoover? Sometimes Madeleine gets pretty stressy about stuff. Like if I drop things or break something, her voice goes really high and she flaps about like a scared bird. A couple of weeks ago I accidentally broke a glass and she screamed as though someone had been shot. I'm convinced that I break more things because her response makes me so nervous. We're in a vicious cycle. I painted a picture about it once. A robot version of Madeleine roaring, with sharp teeth and hair standing on end, then an arrow to me dropping a bomb and an arrow back to her roaring. I made sure the picture was safely hidden behind the boat art.

When she has calmed down enough to finish hoovering, I go and get a snack. There's a Tupperware of chopped carrots and hummus in the fridge. That's Monday's snack. It's not just the meals that are planned, it's the snacks too. Monday is hummus and carrots and then tea is shepherd's pie. We eat at six o'clock on the dot. John gets home at five thirty. Even though we have moved house, literally nothing has changed; the meals are the same and the timings are the same. It's like we have been programmed.

If anything ever happens to mess with the routine, like a parents' evening that clashes with teatime or if John has to go to a work event, Madeleine gets fidgety for days. When we got in at 8 p.m. from the school leavers' play, she had been worrying about it all day and decided we should just have boiled eggs and soldiers for tea and then go straight to bed. As if eating a proper meal after six might cause a catastrophe.

"How was your first day?" she says, when the hoover turns off.

"Fine," I say, dipping a carrot into some hummus.

"Put the carrot down, Fred, and go and change out of your school clothes, please." Her voice is quiet and serious. "We don't want hummus on your new tie, do we?"

I nod and go and get changed. As I'm putting a jumper on and hanging up my blazer I hear the hoover going back on. She must have missed a bit. I get my sketchbook out and start doodling. A giant hoover eating someone.

When John gets home, I hide the drawing and go downstairs. We meet on the stairs.

"Well, how was it, Fred? Your first day as a Gains boy like me?"

"Fine," I say.

"Good stuff. You can tell me all about it at teatime. I'm just getting changed, be down in a tick."

Madeleine is laying the table and when I ask if she wants any help, she swats me away and tells me it's all done. I watch her as she flutters about the kitchen, wiping and organizing the sides. I wonder if she's happy. I start to feel sad for no reason and a bit of panic rises in my chest. Like I should do or say something but I'm not sure what it is. Sometimes I get like this when I feel like I want to talk to my parents about something real. Something more than what's for tea or what homework I have. I don't know what to do about the feeling, so I push it down.

"I'm just going to pop to the beach," I say, suddenly needing to get out of the house.

"Well, tea is at—"

"I know, tea is at six, like it is every day. I'll be here by then, I'm just walking there and back. Getting some fresh air."

Before she can start fretting about me not having time, I get up and leave. I hear her call after me.

"Don't bring a single grain of sand back into this house, I've just hoovered."

You've always "just hoovered", I think. I almost call back and say it out loud but I stop myself.

On the way, I check my tide app and see the tide is out. Perfect. Then I run. When I get to the beach I feel my brain quieten and the world opens up. The sound of the sea and the size of the sky – it's vast. I breathe it in and then clamber up the rocks to my spot, wriggle my bum into the sand to get a good indent and then just sit and stare out at the world.

Ten minutes later I check my watch and scramble back down the rocks. It only feels like I've been sitting there for a minute. I'm not sure what happens to time on the beach; it's like the ocean steals it or something. I run home, dust myself off and open the door just as Madeleine is putting the shepherd's pie on the table. She looks red-faced.

"You're late!" she says, in her highest voice. I look at my watch: 5.59 p.m.

"No, I'm not. I've got one minute."

"If you are not at least five minutes early then you are late," she says.

"That doesn't make sense," I say.

"Stop arguing and sit down."

We all sit and Madeleine dishes out the food. It's silent apart from the clinking of dishes. When we start eating, John says, "So, what teams are you going to join at the Gains, Fred?"

"I don't know," I say, suddenly not feeling too hungry. I don't want to join any teams. I hate sport.

"Just make sure you join something. You need to be on a team. OK?"

I nod and force another mouthful in. I'm definitely not joining the rugby team. It's bad enough that they forced me to do it at my last school. I need to find a sports team that involves sitting in a quiet room and doing very little.

The sound of cutlery is almost deafening in the silence. I sometimes think that my unsaid thoughts and feelings seem so loud that I don't know how they manage to ignore them so well.

Then, as if he's reading my mind, John says, "Sign up tomorrow and you can let me know what you have chosen after school, OK?"

I nod. Looks like I'm joining a team, then. Now I've just got to figure out which one will be least dangerous.

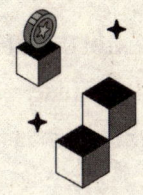

THE TEAM DECISION

Me and Rupert are sitting in our form room trying not to fiddle with the gas taps. It's an immediate detention if the teachers see anyone touching them. I think it's a bit much, giving a load of eleven-year-olds a science form room with the power to create fire and expecting them not to touch anything.

Rupert is really into science. He does experiments at home and I can tell he's super bright. He has glasses that are wonky on his face, and freckles on his nose. His blazer looks even bigger today, as though he's shrunk in the night.

"Why is your blazer so big?" I ask.

"Mum said she never wants to buy me another for the whole time I'm here. She said it was extortionate."

I don't know what extortionate means, and Rupert must be able to tell by my face.

"A rip-off," he whispers, as our form teacher Mr Davies comes in.

"OK, folks, today in form time, it's sign-up day."

Mr Davies is a physics teacher and he wears a tie with a fleece over the top, which seems like a strange combination to me. Like he's about to hike up a mountain to a business meeting.

"We expect all our students to join a club or a team. It builds resilience and helps to make friendships. I will pass the list of enrichment opportunities around and you can put your name next to the ones you would like to sign up for. It's just your top two picks today. Then, when we have the numbers for each club, spaces will open up to join more."

There's a buzz in the classroom. Kids start talking about what they will sign up for. I can hear the girls at the front discussing whether they will do netball or football. The loud boys at the back talk about how they were the top scorer in their last school and that they want to be captain of any team they join. I remember John's words last night and start to worry, because I don't want to be on a team with those boys.

I'm not like them. I don't want to score goals or tries or be a captain of anything.

I turn to Rupert.

"What will you join?" I whisper.

"I think there's a robotics club. What about you?"

"I don't know. John wants me to join a sports team."

He adjusts his glasses and frowns, and I realize too late that I forgot to call him Dad. To try and be normal and not draw attention to my strange family.

"Who's John?"

"He's my dad. I call him John. Don't ask."

"OK. What sports do you like?" he asks, seemingly not too bothered by the John thing.

"That's the problem, I don't like any," I say.

Rupert thinks about it, like he instantly gets it and just needs to find a way to solve it. Then as the list comes around, he says, "How about you come to robotics with me and I'll come to a sport with you? Would that make it better? Then at least you won't be on your own doing something you don't like."

I look at Rupert's kind face and smile.

"Yeah, that would be great."

I have a feeling like maybe this school isn't going to be so bad after all. I've found a friend inside these scary walls. We take the list and look at the options.

As I trace my finger down the list of sports, I move quickly past rugby and football and anything with too much contact. All that's left is cricket and basketball. I have a memory of seeing a cricket ball hit someone in the chin on telly and them having to go to hospital, so I cross that one off in my mind. Basketball it is. At least I'm pretty tall. Before I write my name down, I look at Rupert. There is no way he'll be able to play basketball. He's tiny.

I see him scribbling both our names next to robotics. I don't want to make him do something that he will be terrible at, but he did offer. A small part of me thinks that he might even make me look a bit better, which I feel instantly guilty about. Then on the list a word pops out that I had not seen before. A word that makes me stop and makes me feel a bit giddy.

ART CLUB

That's the club I should be joining. Not basketball or robotics. I don't even know what robotics is. Rupert holds out the pen. My name is already down for robotics and Rupert was so kind to offer to join a sports team with me. I take the pen and hover next to basketball. I can't quite bring myself to write, though. The kids on the table behind tell me to hurry up and stop hogging the sheet.

"What's the matter?" Rupert says, knowing that something is wrong.

"I want to join the art club," I whisper.

"We can do that instead if you like."

"But John – my dad – told me to join a sports team."

He nods, seeing my dilemma. If I choose art, I will have to lie and pretend that I'm on a team. There's no way John would let me get away with doing art instead of sport. But if I do basketball, then I'm not doing the thing I love the most. I feel angry and stuck. The pen moves between the two options, hovering over one and then giving up at the last moment and floating over to the other. The last thing I want to do is lie to my parents but I want to be an artist. I want to draw and paint and let the ideas out of my brain.

Every time I think I've made a decision, I freeze and can't carry it out. I don't know what to choose. I just can't decide.

I need help. What would you do?

If you think I should **choose basketball**, turn to **page 59**.

If you think I should **choose art**, turn to **page 81**.

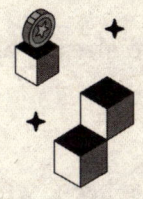

BROWTREE

I stare up at the angry-looking Gains driver, not quite believing that I am about to do what I'm about to do. Then I get a rush of excitement, knowing that for the first time in my life, I am making my own mind up, doing what *I* want. I shake my head slightly to make myself focus.

"No, thank you," I say. "I'm going to Browtree."

He huffs and presses the button to close the doors. I do a tiny shriek and quickly put the jumper on over my shirt and pull the tie off and shove it in my pocket, just as the Browtree bus opens its doors.

"Morning," the bus driver says, as I step on to the bus while trying to contain my excitement. Then he adds, "Can I see your pass, buddy?"

I instantly freeze, my head spinning. I'm not even

sitting down and I've already been caught out. My face goes instantly red.

"My pass?" I ask.

"You should have been sent a pass from the school."

"I've just moved here," I say, hoping to get away with it.

"OK, well, pick one up at school today, otherwise I can't let you on next time."

I nod my head and step past him and into the bus. A sea of red jumpers fills the seats. I feel like everyone is staring, like everyone knows I'm not meant to be here. I find a spot on my own, sit down and look out of the window. I can't help grinning, but I try to make sure no one can see me. I must look pretty strange, sitting on my own and grinning out of the window.

When I can eventually get the daft smile off my face, I look around at the other kids. They are all wearing jeans and trainers with their school jumpers and I glance down at my black school trousers and shiny shoes and know that if I stand any chance of fitting in at Browtree I need to do something pretty quick. I push the collar of my shirt under the neck of the jumper, so hopefully no one can see it, and then I rummage through my bag for my PE kit. I have some trainers but the only other item is some Gains sports shorts and I can't wear them. I silently slip off my shoes and put on the trainers, hoping no one is watching. When I'm done, it's slightly better. The trousers are still embarrassing, though. If I make it through today without being caught then I need to make a plan for tomorrow that means I look a bit less chumpy.

When the bus arrives at the school, I realize that I have no plan of how I am going to get away with this. What will I say when my name isn't on the register? What if Mrs Petts sees me? She knows that Madeleine and John didn't sign me up for Browtree. But then, just as the fear is starting to take hold, I remember that she's not here and I scrunch my fist into a celebration. I've never felt happier about someone being in hospital before. Then I feel bad and send a wish that her operation goes well. I will deal with Mrs Petts when she gets back. For now, I need to get off the bus, get into the school and convince them that I am meant to be there.

There is a smiling teacher standing by the bus when we get off. I go bright red when she looks at me. It feels as though she can immediately tell that I'm in the wrong place.

"Morning, folks, welcome to Browtree. Head over to the tennis courts where we are going to do some games before we split you into your classes."

I breathe a sigh of relief and follow the crowd, trying desperately to blend in.

When we are all standing on the courts, a lady with dyed red hair walks to the middle with a loudspeaker.

"Hello, Year Sevens. My name is Mrs Rumbelow and I am the deputy head here at Browtree. We always like to start the year with a bit of fun to get to know you all. I hope you're ready to make some quick-fire decisions?"

She smiles and there is some chatter and shuffling. I'm not sure that I *am* ready for some quick-fire decisions. I feel like I have already made enough big choices for one day.

"I'm going to make a statement. If you agree, then you run to Mr Haworth, who is your head of year." She points to a man with curly hair who is holding up a big sign that says **Agree**.

"If you disagree with the statement, then you run that way and go and say hello to Miss Gene, who is pastoral support." I turn the other way and see a young-looking woman wearing a spotty skirt, holding a sign that reads **Disagree**.

"These are the people who you can go to any time if you need to chat or ask them anything. OK, you lovely lot, let's have the first statement, shall we?"

We all stand there a bit unsure but excited. This is fun. I bet they're not running around a tennis court at the Gains School! Then she makes the first statement.

"Secondary school is scary."

Some kids immediately run one way or another. A few girls squeal as they run, as if they are being chased. A few kids saunter slowly towards *Disagree*, as if they are far too old for this ridiculous game and far too cool to find anything scary. I look in one direction and then the other. I don't know which way to go. I take a step one way and then a step the other. It definitely feels scary to me but then I am trying to secretly go to a school that I'm not meant to be at, so of course it's scary. A few of us hang around in the middle, unable to commit.

"Five seconds, everyone. There is no right answer." Then she starts counting and that just makes it harder to move. "Five, four, three, two, one. OK, well done. So, to all of you on the *Agree* side, I know that it can often feel overwhelming to start with but I hope that by the end of the day you will be feeling much closer to the *Disagree* side. Please come to any of us if you need help."

I look at the kids all smiling and shuffling, waiting for the next statement. Then I look at Mrs Rumbelow holding up the loudspeaker.

"Statement two: it's easy to make new friends. Go!"

Some more squealing and a lot more chatter. People start discussing it and then head to one side or the other. I'm still frozen in the centre. When most people have made their choice, I see a boy who has been in the middle the whole time like me. I give him an awkward nod.

"It entirely depends on the situation," he says. "These are not binary statements." He looks grumpy and annoyed at the whole thing. I smile.

"I'm just not good at making decisions," I say.

"We shouldn't have to make a decision on such complex topics," he huffs.

"I'm Fred," I say.

"I'm Marco."

When I look up, I catch Mrs Rumbelow looking in our direction and smiling. I smile back and know that the big decision I've made today, the decision to put on the jumper and get on the Browtree bus, was definitely the right one.

"I believe that I am in charge of my own destiny," Mrs Rumbelow calls out.

I smile, for the first time knowing exactly which way to go. I head straight towards the *Agree* sign. This is the school that I want to be at. Now I just have to get away with it.

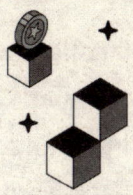

AGREE OR DISAGREE

We keep playing games for a while and everyone seems to relax and start having loads of fun. When we finish a game of counting to ten without interrupting each other Mrs Rumbelow calls us over to a table at the edge of the tennis court.

"Everyone take a name badge and write your name clearly on the front. Then put your name badge on. One of us will come round and tell you which class you are in."

I look around anxiously. This is the first real test. I've got away with it so far purely based on the jumper, which I realize now smells a bit like mushroom soup. I'm not sure how long it was hidden in that bush, but it definitely needs a good wash. Thankfully no one has mentioned the smart trousers or the shirt collar, which keeps poking above the neck of my jumper.

I take a badge and pen and sit down at the side of the court with my back leaning against the mesh fence. I glance up at the groups already forming; friendships and judgements already being made. I've never been one of the most popular kids but I've never been picked on either. At primary it almost felt like I was invisible to everyone else. My mates liked me well enough, although I haven't heard from either Tommy or Frazer since I moved so maybe I was a bit invisible to them too. Maybe that's what happens when you don't really make decisions or have opinions on things; you kind of vanish. I don't want to do that at Browtree. I want people to see me. I want to be known as the kid who can draw. The kid who is cool and creative. I almost wish I could tell everyone that I snuck on to the bus to be here and that I'm rebellious and in charge of my own destiny, but I can't.

I sit and decide if I should write my real name or come up with a fake one. I've always hated the name Timple. It sounds a bit too much like simple. I start thinking about all the names I could have:

FRED BLAZE
FRED FIRE
FRED BEST
FRED AMAZING
FRED COOL

Then I laugh to myself, realizing that they are all completely ridiculous and will definitely get me caught.

Marco comes and sits next to me and sees me smiling at the empty name badge.

"Have you forgotten your own name?" he asks in a serious way, which makes me question if he's joking.

"Of course not!" I say, and write FRED TIMPLE in big, clear letters.

Maybe it's best to stick to my own name anyway. It could get complicated, remembering to answer to a different name. I just need to convince the teachers that I should be here.

I look over at Marco's badge: **MARCO MARVEL**.

"Is that seriously your name?" I ask.

"Of course it is," he says. "Why on earth would I make that up?"

Maybe I could have got away with being Fred Fire after all.

Miss Gene heads our way and looks at our name badges. She hands Marco a map of the school and a timetable.

"You are in Ash Class. Your form room is in the food tech block – 5D. When the bell goes you can head straight there. If you need anything or have any concerns, questions or worries then you can come to pastoral and find me. It's just here." She smiles kindly and points to the map. I wonder if she has said this to everyone or if she thinks Marco looks like he might need some extra help in this new school.

Marco is definitely the kind of kid who would be bullied. You can spot them a mile off. He's a mixture of awkward but confident and he looks like he would be more comfortable in a shirt and tie than in his Browtree jumper. I can tell he's super bright just from the way he speaks. Part of me wonders if we should do a swap. If I should tell him to get on the other bus and he can take my place at the Gains School. Miss Gene interrupts my thoughts.

"Fred, I can't seem to find you on my list." I look at her and the lies seem to flow out of my mouth without me even having to think.

"We just moved, miss. Mrs Petts showed me around last week. Madeleine—" I stop myself; I don't need her thinking I'm weird. "When my mum called her to tell her that I would like to enrol, she was getting ready for her operation."

I'm so impressed with myself. I sound so believable.

"Oh, I see. Well, I will add you to the list and get the secretary to follow it up. We may need to give your mum a call to confirm."

"OK," I squeak, trying to seem relaxed. "What class should I go to?"

"How about you two stick together, eh? I will put you in Ash Class with Marco."

I breathe a sigh of relief. That's the first hurdle over. My name is on the list and I have a class. I look at Marco, who has taken what looks like an eight-sided Rubik's cube out of his bag and is clicking away at it.

The bell rings and we both stand up, Marco still twisting and clicking like a cricket. His hands moving at insect speed.

"Do you know which way we need to go?" I ask, looking at the map Miss Gene gave me.

"Yes, follow me."

Then he completes the eight-sided Rubik's cube and holds it out to me.

"Can you mix it up for me again, please?"

"Yeah," I say, following him as he walks ahead. I'm not entirely sure that I want to get stuck with Marco. If I want to be a new, better version of myself at Browtree, I'm not convinced Marco will help me to stand out in the way that I want to. Then I look down at my smart trousers, adjust my collar and wonder if actually we look perfect for each other.

I will just keep my head down and find a way to make friends and blend in tomorrow when I can wear some joggers and ditch the shirt.

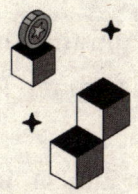

THE WHERE-TO-SIT DECISION

After I have muddled up the Rubik's cube and handed it back to Marco we get to our form room. I peer through the door and see a whole mix of different kids. Shy ones sitting alone at desks, twiddling with pens. Groups who clearly already know each other, laughing and checking that everyone can see how much fun they are having. Laddy lads who try and dominate the room, boys who look like they are permanently embarrassed and everyone in between.

I know that if I walk in with Marco then we will be stuck together. I see a sign for the toilets on the opposite side of the corridor and stand frozen, wondering what to do. Marco walks through the classroom door and turns back to me.

"Are you coming?" he says.

I vaguely gesture towards the toilets; he shrugs and heads into the classroom. I turn and dash into the toilets.

I put the lid down and sit on the seat. My head is swimming. I can't believe I'm actually here, my name on the register and about to have form time in my new, secret school. I scratch my neck where the itchy shirt collar sits and unzip my bag. Maybe the PE shorts are no good but perhaps I can ditch the shirt and wear my Gains PE shirt. When I pull it out I see the Gains emblem embroidered on the front. I'm so relieved that I am not in that scary building right now. I turn the shirt inside out and quickly strip off. If I keep my jumper on all day, this will be fine and the annoying, itchy collar will be gone.

By the time I get back to the classroom most of the tables are full. I scan the room to see what my options are. When I see a space next to Marco, who is now reading some huge textbook, I feel bad that deep down the reason I went and hid in the toilets was so that I wouldn't be stuck with him.

The only other seat in the room is next to a skinny boy with two shaved lines in his hair. He is standing on his chair and doing some sort of song and dance. I can imagine Madeleine's voice in my head: *Well, he looks like trouble.* I know that she would want me to make the sensible choice and sit with Marco. She would fully approve of him and his gigantic textbook. Who even reads textbooks before lessons have actually started?

I look at the two seats: the two different options in front of me. I don't want to always do what my parents would want, or what seems like the "right" choice. That's why I'm here in the first place. I want to make different decisions. Live a life that is my own. Maybe it will be more interesting, more exciting to sit with a boy who sings and dances on the furniture. Maybe I will have the best time if I become friends with him. But then maybe I will be more likely to get caught. I have to remember that I can't get into trouble here. No way.

I look over at Marco, who catches my eye and moves his bag from the chair next to him, as if it's just a fact that I will sit there. As if he's now in charge of my life.

Argh. I don't know what to do. I take one step towards Marco and then one towards the singer. Then I stop. Yet again frozen, as if this is the biggest choice of my life. I know that it's only a seat in form room, it's not a big deal. So why does it feel so big?

Why does every decision in my life always feel so important? From whether to eat an apple or a banana to what chair to sit in, it always feels like picking the wrong one means the end of the world.

As my heartbeat thumps in my chest and I start to sweat into my itchy trousers, a teacher appears behind me and makes me startle like a terrified animal.

"I'm Mrs Machen. Sit yourselves down and we will go through the register," she says. I turn and see a big lady with an apron on. She looks more like someone's nan than a teacher. I stand there waiting for her to tell me where to sit, so I can give up on the idea of free will. When she doesn't, and she just heads to the front of the class and waits for me with a smile on her face, I feel even more panicky. The whole class is staring at me: I know that I'm now drawing attention to myself.

I don't know what to do. I need help. What would you do?

If you think I should **sit with Marco**, turn to **page 123**.

If you think I should **sit with the chair singer**, turn to **page 103**.

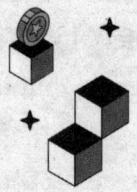

RUPERT'S HOUSE

"Hurry up!" comes the angry hiss from the table behind.

Rupert looks sadly at me, as though he really understands how hard it is.

"Maybe there will be space in art club as well. Sir said spaces come up later on."

I nod sadly. I'm rubbish at lying anyway. John would know if I wasn't on a sports team. That's all he will ask me about every teatime. I won't be able to lie convincingly enough. I sigh and write my name and then Rupert's next to basketball and hand the paper to the desk behind.

The impatient hand of the girl behind snatches it from me.

"Finally," she huffs.

I feel a jolt of anxiety lurch through my body as the paper leaves my grasp, but it's too late. I've done it now.

"Have you ever played basketball before, Rupert?" I ask.

"I'm not even five foot yet. What do you think? Have you ever programmed a robot?"

"Nope," I say.

"Well, I guess we'll both learn something new."

He doesn't seem worried at all, about anything. I wonder how he does it. I can't imagine being at this big new school and feeling confident enough to do something that I know I would be terrible at. I can't even imagine feeling confident enough to make a simple decision.

The rest of the day, me and Rupert stick together. At lunch, when I don't know what to have, I just copy him and we both sit there with identical lunches and he chatters about his older brother and some show on TV that he loves. I spend the whole time checking for danger.

I do this a lot, especially in new places. I scan the room and see what could hurt me or where I might need to run for a quick escape. There are a lot of dangers in the lunch hall. Mainly human ones in the shape of boys who want to make themselves look better by making someone else look worse, and girls who think being cruel is the same as being funny. There are also the physical dangers of towers of empty trays falling and landing on me, chairs being pulled back and screeching loudly at random, an angry dinner lady who looks ready to blow. There are two exits, the main double doors and a smaller door at the back of the hall. The smaller one is the one I'll use if there's a fire, which is also a danger, as we are next to the kitchen.

I once asked Madeleine if this was a normal thing to do. If everyone scans for danger like I do, and she said that it sounded very sensible to her. I'm not so sure, though. I look at Rupert yammering away about some science teacher. He has not even noticed the kid sitting right next to him who has spilled his drink all over the floor, making it a definite slip hazard, let alone the millions of other dangers in the room. I try to listen to what he's saying but I can't help feeling sad. I wish I could relax and be a bit happier like he is.

At the end of the day, when the bell goes, I feel a wash of relief flood through me. I made it through another day and nothing catastrophic has happened. I managed to dodge a negative in maths when the teacher nearly caught me doodling a picture of him. Luckily his stinky breath warned me that he was behind me just in time for me to rip out the sheet from my book. I put it in the bin by his desk, half hoping that he would see it. To get my own back on him and all the other scary teachers in this school. Maybe they should know how scary they are. Maybe they already do and they just don't care. I completely forgot that I had instinctively added my initials at the bottom like I do with all my drawings.

When we head to the bus bay, Rupert says, "Do you want to come over to mine?"

I'm slightly surprised and not sure what to say. There is such a simplicity to Rupert. Everything seems so easy. I'm not sure if I can go to his house, though. It's not been planned and Madeleine will be expecting me home. Does he mean come now or another day? What about tea? It's Tuesday so Madeleine will have already made the lasagne. I would like to go, though. I'm not sure what to say.

In the silence, while my brain whirrs at a million miles an hour, Rupert pats my arm.

"I live just down the road," he says. "Why don't you ring your mum – what do you call her?"

"Madeleine," I say, feeling happier now he seems to be telling me what to do.

"Call Madeleine and ask if it's OK. My parents can drop you back later."

"What about tea?" I ask. "How do you know your parents will drop me back?"

"Have tea at mine or we can take you back before if that's better. My parents will always drop friends home."

Then, when I don't do anything, he says, "Call her and ask."

"OK," I say, getting my phone out.

Predictably Madeleine gets very flustered at the idea and while she is flapping and I'm trying not to get stressed, I see my bus pull out of the bus bay.

"Well, I have missed my bus now," I say.

"Fred!" she shrieks down the phone.

I eventually talk her round and we make a plan that I will be back by six, so the lasagne is not wasted. She also makes me vow to never "dump her in it like this last minute again". Although I'm not sure how I have exactly dumped her in anything.

When we get to Rupert's house, I can't quite believe my eyes. There are about twenty bikes in the front garden. Some of them look completely broken and others look pretty good.

"My brother likes fixing bikes," he says, as he sees me looking at them.

In the porch, the entire floor is taken up with shoes. Piles and piles of wellies, walking boots and trainers. Rupert kicks his off on to one of the piles. I take mine off and carefully balance them on top of the cleanest pair of trainers I can find, wondering whether I will ever find them again.

"How many brothers and sisters do you have?" I ask.

"Two brothers, two sisters," he says and then calls out, "Hi, Mum."

As he steps over what looks like some kind of animal cage, I follow him and try and catch a glimpse of what's inside.

"It's a rat," he says matter-of-factly. "My sister Alice is into rodents."

I jump away from the cage and he laughs.

"She has ten of them."

I'm starting to freak out. I'm not sure I can be in a house with ten rats. But also I'm intrigued. What kind of parents let their kids collect old bikes and rats? I have to see more, so I follow Rupert into the kitchen, which at first glance, apart from being messy and chaotic, is disappointingly normal looking. Then I see what's wrong with the picture. Standing chopping carrots at the kitchen counter is who I assumed to be Rupert's mum, but when she turns round, she looks younger than me. She can only be about eight and she is standing on a little stool cooking tea. There are some pots boiling on the hob and the oven is turned on and the smell of baking fills the kitchen. Rupert opens the fridge and throws me a carton of juice and then gets some crisps out of a cupboard.

"What are we having, Jessie?" he asks, as he looks into a pan.

"Fajitas with wedges, salsa verde and corn on the cob," she says, as though she's on *MasterChef*.

"This is Jessie, she loves cooking. This is Fred."

"Hi," she calls, as she turns on a whizzer and the room fills with sound.

As we leave the kitchen, I turn to Rupert.

"How old is she? Should she be in the kitchen alone like that?"

"She's nine. She's a better cook than the rest of us.

Mum says it's better to leave her to it or she gets angry like Gordon Ramsay."

On our way upstairs we step over a small boy who is surrounded by comics. Rupert ruffles his hair and the boy swats him away, so we carry on up the stairs.

Rupert's room is calm compared to the rest of the house. There are shelves with science kits and mechanical-looking objects all neatly lined up. I go and look at all the strange items and immediately get ideas for drawings.

This house is something else. It's loud and chaotic and the kids seem so different. They know who they are and they are allowed to be themselves. It's kind of amazing. I don't know whether to feel jealous or impressed.

After Rupert has shown me all the things on the shelves, we have a quick game of Uno and then I look at my watch and realize it's time to go. I don't want to ask Rupert, as it seems rude to tell him that he needs to get his mum to drive me home. I've not even met her yet. But he sees me check the time and knows.

"Come on, then. Maybe next time you can stay for tea. Jessie is pretty good."

I nod and smile. "I'd like that," I say.

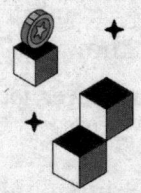

THE BASKETBALL TEAM

When I get home, Madeleine and John are already sitting at the table. I check my watch and it's only five to six, so I'm not late, but they don't look happy.

"Is this how it's going to be now that you are at secondary school?" Madeleine says, as she brings out the lasagne. "Last-minute phone calls and missing buses?"

"I made a friend," I say, knowing that the slightly whining tone in my voice is not going to help.

"A little more notice next time, please, Fred. Go and wash your hands, I don't know where you've been," she says, as she finishes bringing things to the table.

"I've been to Rupert's house," I say. I want to tell them all about it. About the mess and the bikes and the tiny chef. But I know they will just huff and disapprove and maybe never let me go there again, so I don't say anything.

"Your mother just wants some respect," John says. I don't understand how I've been disrespectful, so I keep quiet. Then he takes a big drink and changes the subject.

"So, what teams did you sign up to, Fred?"

The atmosphere shifts a bit and I feel so glad that I didn't choose art club. That I don't have to lie and maybe I can please him for a change.

"Basketball," I say hopefully.

John takes a bite of his lasagne and waits. Then: "Anything else? What about rugby or cricket?"

I sigh. I should have known it would not be good enough.

"What's wrong with basketball?" I ask.

"It's a bit showy and American, if you ask me. What else did you choose?"

I pause, knowing that I've let them down again. Maybe I should have just chosen art and lied. I can't win whatever I do.

"Robotics," I say. "Me and Rupert are doing it together. It's like science and computing."

"I know what robotics is, Fred. It's not a sport,

though. I thought we decided you would join a team."

"I did," I say. "Basketball."

Suddenly I don't feel so hungry, but I will have to empty my plate before I'm allowed to leave the table.

"Well, it's not really what I had in mind, but it's your life, I guess."

It doesn't feel like it's my life, though. It feels like it's theirs. Like they are making every single decision for me and I have no control over anything. I didn't want to go to that stupid school. I didn't want to join any team. I wanted to be sitting in the art room. I'm so fed up of doing everything for everyone else.

I shovel the food into my mouth and don't say another word for the whole of tea. When I am finally allowed to clear the plates, I do it as quickly as I can.

"Can I go to the beach?" I mumble when the dishes are all stacked in the dishwasher. Madeleine sighs.

"Please," I add.

"You have been out all afternoon and now you want to go out again?"

I don't know what to say to this, so I just stand there. John gets up and joins Madeleine.

"I think you should go to your room, Fred, and think about your life choices. The beach won't help you with that."

"But—"

"But nothing," John shouts. "That's enough, Fred."

I look at their faces and a huge wave of anger surges through me. I haven't done anything wrong. I literally haven't done a single thing wrong. I was home on time. I joined a sports team. I went to his scary school and I even made a friend. I hate them. I hate them. I want to live in a house with comic books all over the stairs, where I'm allowed to paint pictures and put them on my bedroom walls. I hate this house and I hate my parents. All of these thoughts flood through my mind, but I can't say any of them. It's as though all my true thoughts have been silenced.

I walk out of the kitchen and trudge up the stairs. I can't believe I have to go back to that school and do basketball tomorrow and all for nothing. At least Rupert will be there with me. Maybe from now on I need to make decisions that are right for me and nobody else.

As I walk into my tidy, characterless room I can't help myself. I throw the duvet on the floor and turn every single picture upside down. I take my neatly folded clothes out of the drawers and stamp them into the pristine carpet. Then I tape every single one of my pictures on to the walls, knowing that Madeleine will be furious and not caring one bit.

As I look around at my colourful walls I smile. Bring on the next big decision; this time I'll be ready for it.

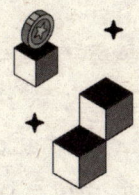

THE BULLYING DECISION

The next day at school Rupert leans over to me in form time.

"I watched some basketball last night on YouTube. I'm probably going to be terrible at it!" He smiles, but I can see there are real nerves behind the smile too.

"Don't worry, I've got you. Anyway, tomorrow is robotics, and believe me I'll be terrible at that. It's only one lunchtime, how bad can it be?"

He smiles again and nods and we both stop talking in time for the register to start.

When the bell goes for lunch break, we head straight to the changing rooms and as we walk in, I instantly know that this is not going to be good. The smell of boys and sweat hits us and I see Rupert's nose scrunch up. When we put our bags down a group of absolutely massive lads stare at us for what feels like for ever.

When eventually they go back to play fighting and hurling insults at each other, I whisper to Rupert, "They can't be Year Sevens, they must be here for something else."

"I know! Look at the size of them," Rupert whispers back.

It becomes clear when we go into the gym that they are in fact Year Sevens. *Huge* Year Sevens.

We all stand in the gym and wait for the teacher. There are three clear groups. The giant, loud, staring boys from the changing room. They are the rulers and it's obvious they will be the best at basketball. It's weird how you can just tell who'll be good at something before you even start. Then there are a group of smaller, more normal-looking boys who seem like they don't know each other but who have ended up standing together for some kind of comfort or protection. Then there are the outsiders like me and Rupert. Just random boys dotted around on their own.

It feels like a nature documentary. It's clear, if we were animals, which ones would be the hunted and who would be doing the hunting. There is definitely safety in a group. I edge towards the smaller boys but don't make it to safety before the hunters smell blood.

A boy with a shaved head finds a basketball in the corner and bounces it menacingly towards us. As he passes the occasional lone boy, he twitches and moves towards them as quick as a flash, pretending he's about to throw the ball their way. They inevitably flinch, ready to try and catch the imaginary throw, which makes the rest of the hunters howl with laughter. It's amazing how many times the trick works. He makes five different boys flinch, the howls of laughter rising with each strike.

By the time he reaches us, I'm praying that the teacher appears. I know that Rupert will draw attention because of his size. He's smaller than everyone in the room by a long way.

"Hey, shorty," the boy says, bouncing the ball between his legs. Then he shouts, "Catch!" He really looks as though he is about to throw the ball.

Rupert, who has been watching the events unfold, believes, like all of us, that the boy is toying with him. That he won't actually throw the ball. He just wants yet another reaction. So Rupert stands firm and doesn't even flicker. I feel a moment of pride when

I see his lack of reaction but it vanishes when I see the ball flying through the air, as if in slow motion, towards his face.

It happens so quickly, I don't have time to warn him. The ball hits Rupert square in the nose, so quickly and so violently that time seems to speed up and go into technicolour at the moment of impact.

Rupert flies backwards and at the same moment the voice of the teacher can be heard shouting from near the gym door.

"What is going on here, boys?"

I turn to the voice and I see the bald, shushy lady from the first day. She has a whistle around her neck and a stopwatch in her hand. No! She can't be the coach.

The boy with the shaved head instantly transforms and he manages to make himself look like a normal human child and not a hunting beast.

"Sorry, miss. I was trying to help everyone warm up and this little lad didn't put his hands out to catch. I did warn him, didn't I, lads?"

The other lads obviously all agree and nod their heads. Rupert's nose has at this point started gushing with blood. The bald lady shakes her head and ushers Rupert out to the toilet.

By the time he comes back, he looks a little sheepish and I can see dried blood all over his face. We've done some passing, dribbling and shooting, and now we are moving on to a game. I'm actually decent and scored the most shots out of everyone. I breathe a sigh of relief when the boy with the shaved head holds his fist out for a bump as I score a particularly nice three-pointer. I know that this means they won't hunt me down.

I'm starting to think I could enjoy this sport but when Rupert comes back and gets put on my team, I see the shaved boy's eyes roll and his head shake. For the rest of the game they humiliate Rupert. They dance around him with the ball and throw it just out of his reach. They make him dizzy and call him names just quietly enough that the angry bald coach can't hear.

When we get back to the changing rooms, Rupert looks broken.

"What's your name?"

It's the shaved boy, and he is talking to me.

"Fred."

"I'm Callum. You're decent."

"Cheers," I say, trying not to look at him and instead glancing apologetically at Rupert.

"Why don't you ditch your little girlfriend, who can't even catch, and come and sit with us, Fred?"

I panic. What did he just say?

I go to say no. To shake my head and think of all the words I should say.

"Thank you, but Rupert is my friend and I need to make sure he is OK after what you all have just done to him."

But the words and gestures don't come and I just stay silent.

It felt so nice out there being good at something and these boys have noticed. They want me to be one of them. Maybe this is the moment that I can change my whole school life. Become less of a victim. Become the son my dad wants me to be.

My brain starts scrambling. I look at Rupert's face and he puts his head down towards his shoelaces. He can't help me with this one; I'm on my own. I loved going to Rupert's house last night, seeing the wonderful chaos of his family. But it's only been two days. It's not like we've been best buddies for ever or anything, is it? Kids change friends loads when they start new schools; it's just the way it is. Anyway, if I go and hang out with Callum and his mates, I can still be friends with Rupert. I can sit next to him in form time and I can still go to robotics. It's no big deal making different friends. Why am I being so intense about it?

I'm about to say yes and then I look back to Rupert and his nose is bleeding again. These aren't just more new friends, though, are they? These are kids who are mean. They will be mean to Rupert and if I don't hang out with them, they will probably be mean to me. Can I ditch my new friend to save myself and try and impress John? Or should I just be a good friend to Rupert even though I've only just met him? I can't decide. I have no idea what to do. What would you do?

If you would **join Callum and his friends**, turn to **page 163**.

If you would **tell Callum that you're staying with Rupert**, turn to **page 141**.

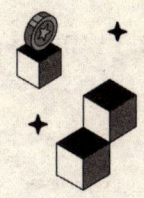

THE ART ROOM

"Hurry up!" comes the angry hiss from the table behind.

Rupert looks at me sadly, as though he really understands how hard it is.

"Maybe there will be space in art as well. Sir said spaces come up later on."

I'm rubbish at lying anyway. John would know if I wasn't on a team. That's all he'll ask me about every teatime. I won't be able to lie convincingly enough.

As I bring the pen down towards the paper to sign up for basketball the wind blows through the open window and the sign-up sheet lands on the floor. As I pick it up I notice that art club is happening today. This lunchtime I could be drawing. I've not even seen the art room yet. I want to go there and I want to go today!

I quickly write my name and then Rupert's name next to art. Rupert leans over and smiles before handing the sheet to the table behind.

"I'm pretty relieved you chose that one, to be honest. I think I would be horrendous at basketball!"

"Why didn't you tell me?" I say. He could have made my decision way easier.

"I didn't want you to get in trouble with your parents on my behalf. Anyway, you're coming to robotics with me, so I would have done it. It just could have gone very wrong. Me and sport don't really mix."

"Well, it's a good job I changed my mind at the last minute. Who knows what I've saved you from."

"Sometimes I try to picture alternate lives," Rupert says. "Not sure I want to picture that one!"

I think about this. The idea of alternate lives. About what would be happening in another version of my life where I made different choices.

"I get a bit stuck making decisions," I say. "I guess it's the fear of not knowing the alternate life and which one is better."

"My mum says there is no such thing as better or worse, there just is."

I'm not entirely sure what this means but I quite like the sound of it. Then the bell goes for our first lesson.

I manage to drag myself through the morning, knowing that at lunch I will get to be myself. I sit quietly through maths as a very grumpy man shouts at us about equations. As he walks between the desks, still shouting, even though no one has done anything wrong, I can't stop myself from doodling a tiny picture on the corner of my book. Something that I want to draw at lunchtime. A teacher robot, whose head is exploding with metal numbers and symbols, smoke coming out of the ears. The grumpy man's voice is getting louder but I'm too immersed in the drawing and thoughts of art club to notice.

"The expressions on the two sides of the equals sign are called the left-hand side and right-hand side of the equation."

He stops further up the row of desks.

"Very often the right-hand side of an equation is assumed to be zero."

As he says the word "zero" I see a shower of spit land on my page and get a waft of his acidic breath. It's too late. He is leaning over my book and as I quickly cover the drawing with my arm, I know that I'm not quick enough.

He whips the book from under my arm and holds it up for the class to see.

"Day two as a Gains student and he doesn't need to learn a thing. He can doodle. He is bored, is he? He thinks maths is beneath him, does he? Well, young man, you will not go far in this school with that attitude. What is your name?"

"Fred."

"Fred what?"

"Fred Timple."

"Fred Timple WHAT?"

He is really shouting now and even more spit and smell are coming out of his mouth. I don't know what he wants from me. I'm frozen, not knowing if I should look at him or not.

After what feels like an eternity, in which I start sweating like crazy, he says in a quiet and even more menacing voice, "Fred Timple, sir."

I nod.

"Say it, then, Fred Timple."

"Fred Timple, sir?"

"Finally," he says. "One negative for you, young man. Do not let me catch you drawing in my class again."

He tears the doodle out of my book, throws the

book back on my desk, dumping the picture into the bin. When I pick up the book, my hands are shaking. I look at Rupert and he looks sad and shrugs.

All because I was doodling again. If John and Madeleine found out about this, they would be so cross. I can't believe I chose art and now I have to lie to them and I know how much they hate my doodles. Oh god, what have I done?

When the lunch bell finally rings, I close my eyes for a moment. I forget the lies that I will have to tell and I wait for Rupert at the door.

"Now, let's go somewhere you won't get into trouble for drawing!" he says.

"Yes, please," I say, and we head down the long hallway.

When we eventually find the art room, it's tucked away at the end of a corridor beyond some toilets. As soon as I peek in through the door, it feels like a different world. The fear that I feel in the rest of the school vanishes as I see the pastels and paints and pictures hanging from string across the room.

There's a lady sitting at the desk and she looks up and smiles.

"Are you here for art club?"

We nod.

"Well, help yourself. I'm Miss Nolan, the art teacher. You can use anything you want and do anything you want. Be as creative as you like."

Then she sits back down and eats a sandwich. I look around; there is no one else here. We take our bags off and sit at a table next to the paints. I only have an hour, so I want to get started.

When I have my paper ready, I notice that Rupert has not moved.

"What are you going to do?" I ask.

"Not sure really, I'm not very good at drawing."

"You don't have to draw. Look, there is clay, straws or all sorts of things over there. Why don't you build something? Like one of your robotic things?"

"Because it won't work."

"But it will look cool," I say, and then start painting.

He starts gathering things from around the classroom.

The hour flies by and we barely speak but it's the happiest I have felt since I've been at this school.

As we are packing up to leave, the teacher looks at my painting and smiles.

"That's impressive. You are welcome any time, boys. The art room isn't really used enough, so I'm happy for you to come any lunchtime."

"What day is robotics?" I ask Rupert, knowing that I will be here every single other day of the week.

"Not until Thursday," he says. "Shall we come here tomorrow? It was fun."

I nod.

Maybe the Gains School isn't going to be so bad after all.

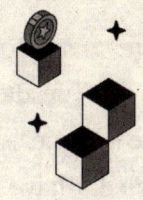

THE LIES

I almost forget the lies that I'm going to have to tell when I get home but when the bell goes at the end of the day I get a jolt of worry about seeing John and Madeleine. I've never been any good at lying. I get really conscious of my face and start doing strange things with my eyes and mouth. Either keeping everything way too still or moving everything far too much. Either way I look suspicious.

When we head to the bus bay, Rupert says, "Do you want to come over to mine?"

I'm slightly surprised and I'm not sure what to say. There is such a simplicity to Rupert. Everything seems so easy. I'm not sure if I can go to his house, though. It's not been planned and Madeleine will be expecting me. Does he mean come now or another day? What about tea? It's Tuesday, so Madeleine will have already made the lasagne. Also, I have got to tell them what team I joined. I have to start the lies.

I would like to go. I'm not sure what to say. In the silence, while my brain whirrs at a million miles an hour, Rupert says, "I live just down the road. Why don't you ring your mum – do you call her?"

"Madeleine," I say, feeling happier now he seems to be telling me what to do.

"Call Madeleine and ask if it's OK. My parents can drop you back later."

Then, when I don't do anything, he says, "Call her and ask."

"OK," I say, getting my phone out.

As soon as Madeleine answers, I know that I'm in trouble. Her voice is so shrill I have to pull the phone away from my ear.

"A negative on day two, Fred?"

It sounds like she's crying.

"What?" I say, not knowing what on earth is going on.

"I have the app!" she wails. "You got a negative in maths for doodling. I'm so disappointed in you, Fred."

"Oh," I say, knowing that I'm definitely not going to Rupert's now.

As she is telling me how cross John will be and what a terrible start to my secondary school career it is, I see my bus close its doors. I run towards it and I'm sure the grumpy driver sees me and rolls his eyes, but the bus pulls away. I close my eyes, take a big breath in and tip my head back. I can hear Madeleine, still in full flow, on the end of the phone. The last thing I can tell her now is that I missed the bus. I put the phone back to my ear.

"I'm really sorry. See you in a bit." And before she hangs up, I say quickly, "The bus is a bit late so I might be a while."

She sighs loudly down the phone and I hang up. Rupert studies me closely.

"You in trouble?"

"Yup, she knows about the negative in maths."

"How are you going to get home?"

I shrug. I could walk but it will take ages. I look at the map on my phone: it says it will take an hour. She'll be fuming if I take that long.

Then Rupert pats me on the back.

"I've got an idea. How about you bike it?"

"I haven't got a bike."

"I have. Come on!" he says and dashes off in the opposite direction. I can't think of anything better to do, so I just follow.

When we get to Rupert's house, I can't quite believe my eyes. There are about twenty bikes in the front garden. Some of them look completely broken and others look pretty good.

"My brother likes fixing bikes," he says, as he sees me looking at them.

"Pick one."

"I can't just take one of your brother's bikes!" I say.

"He can't use this many bikes. He doesn't even ride them, he just likes fixing them. Anyway, you can bring it back."

I look at all the bikes and choose a red one that definitely has brakes and pumped-up tyres.

"Where does he get them all?" I ask.

"Mum finds them for free on Facebook or in skips. People just give them away."

The whole garden is completely covered in bike parts.

"Doesn't your mum mind all this mess?"

"No, she's not really bothered, as long as he keeps it outside. Once he snuck one into his bedroom and there were oily footprints all the way up the stairs.

The rule is no bikes in the house now. He wants to fix bikes for a job so he's got to learn somewhere, hasn't he?"

"I guess so," I say. "My mum – Madeleine – would never ever let me do this."

"Why?" Rupert asks.

"The mess."

"You should see the rest of our house, it's chaos!"

"I think Madeleine is terrified of chaos. That's why she won't let me do art, it's messy with no rules, she doesn't understand it. That's what I love about it."

Rupert looks sad for a moment.

"Have you told her that? Explained why you love it?"

I shake my head.

"I can't really speak to my parents about stuff like that," I say.

"Maybe it's worth a try."

I check the route home and it says it will take twenty minutes by bike. I will be a bit later than the bus but hopefully not too much to get into even more trouble. Then I have a thought.

"How will I explain the bike?" I say to Rupert. "She thinks I'm on the bus."

Rupert has an idea and smiles.

"Give me a backy and then I can ride it home after."

"Really? You would do that for me?"

"Of course. It'll be fun. Squidge up."

He dumps his bag in the house and I get a glimpse through the door. A boy is sitting on the stairs surrounded by stuff and there's the sound of pots and pans coming from the kitchen. It looks messy, busy and fun. Then he closes the door and climbs on the back of the bike.

"I've never given anyone a backy before," I tell him.

"Well, now's as good a time as any!"

I push off and we get off to a wobbly start. Rupert laughs and slowly I get some speed up, getting used to the weight.

"Go faster!" Rupert shouts. "Madeleine is waiting."

I pump the pedals and the wind rushes over my face. I feel free. Even though I'm in trouble and I have to lie to my parents, in this moment, rushing down the back lanes with Rupert whooping on the back, I feel totally free.

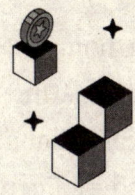

THE ANGER DECISION

I let Rupert off at the bottom of our road so Madeleine doesn't spy me out of the window. Once I have waved him off, I flatten my hair and try to make myself look more like I have been on a bus rather than whizzing through the cold air at high speed.

When I get to the house, I feel myself shrink slightly. The freedom that I felt today in art club and on the bike is ebbing away. As I walk through the door, the house is silent. I don't want to have to deal with this. I can't tell the truth, I can't explain that the maths teacher was a power-crazed nugget and that I didn't want to be in the school in the first place.

I quietly close the door and take my shoes off. I'm planning on sneaking upstairs before Madeleine even knows that I'm home, to put off seeing her sad, stressed face until teatime, but as I'm putting my shoes in my allocated shoe hole, I look up and she's there. Puffy-eyed and arms folded. From her expression, you would think I'd been arrested for murder, not caught doodling. I sigh, puffing out my cheeks, and start to follow her into the kitchen.

"You may well sigh, Fred. How do you think I feel? Upstairs until your father is home. I don't even want to look at you."

A rush of relief washes over me. I can hide in my bedroom away from all her intensity. I walk up the stairs, trying not to run or make too much noise or do anything that might annoy her more.

I hear John get back and then the low rumble of their voices but no words. I can tell from the tone they are talking about me. At five to six I have to go and face them. The lasagne is on the table and they're both standing in the kitchen waiting for me. I sit down in the silence and they stay standing. The pause is huge. I desperately try to think of what they want from me. Do they want me to go back upstairs? To stand up again? To cry? Beg? I remember other times they have been angry with me and try to remember what I did to fix it.

The time I drew a skeleton all over my body in Sharpie, they made me take all the permanent markers in the house to a charity shop and promise that I would never "mark my body in such an obscene way" again. I thought it looked pretty cool actually, but it did take a few weeks to come off properly.

The time I used all of John's printer paper to make a flick book, I had to do gardening jobs to save enough money to buy him some more. I don't know what I can do as penance for this.

As I sit there, wishing that I could make it all go away, John breaks the silence.

"What have you got to say to your mother?"

"Sorry?" I say quickly.

She makes a sound like a sob and then they both sit down at the table and the lecture begins.

They spend the entire time telling me how the things I do now will map out my future. How if I make the wrong choices at this age, my whole life will be ruined. How one negative for doodling can turn into detentions, then expulsions and then a life of crime. By the end of tea, I feel broken. Maybe they're right. Maybe this is as big a deal as they are making it and I am the worst son in the world. I stack the dishes in silence and then as I'm heading to the door John asks the question that I've been dreading.

"What team did you sign up for, Fred?"

My face instantly goes red and my eyes start randomly blinking. I put my head down and whisper, "Basketball."

"Good. At least that's one half-decent choice you made today. Although basketball is a bit showy and American, if you ask me."

I nod and try to walk as calmly as I can out of the door. By the time I'm in my bedroom I'm shaking.

I take out my phone to see a message from Rupert:

> How was it?

> Bad

> Well, the bike ride was fun! Shall we do it again tomorrow? And shall we go back to art at lunch?

I smile to myself. All the scary words and negative futures that Madeleine and John painted for me at tea seem to vanish as I think about riding the bike and being in the art room. I look at my phone and type:

👍

The next day at lunch we head straight to the art room. I'm finding my way around the huge corridors now and it still feels scary but at least I know where I'm going and I have Rupert by my side. When we get there, everything is different. There are two teachers taking all the pegged-up pictures down and the art teacher is standing at the back of the room, looking annoyed.

"Hi, boys," she says when she sees us. "I'm sorry but there is a change of plan. One of the science rooms has a leak and so they have decided to move some science lessons down here."

"What about art?"

"We will be sharing the space for a while, just until things are fixed."

"What about art club?" I ask.

"Not enough people signed up, so they are discontinuing it."

"That's not fair!" Rupert says, as though he can read my mind and say the thing I wouldn't have the guts to say.

"I know," the teacher says. "I'm going to fight for it, believe me, but I don't have much hope."

Then the other teachers start rearranging the tables and she dashes over to rescue some sculptures.

As we watch the room being stripped of all its character, I feel something inside my belly rising and tears stinging in my eyes. How dare they take this away from me? This is the one thing that I liked about this horrible school. How will I ever be an artist if there is no room to do art in? If the only things people seem to care about are science and maths and being on a sports team?

The teachers leave the room and Rupert pats me on the back.

"That's pretty rubbish, Fred. I'm sorry."

I nod, trying to ignore the feeling of tears in my eyes. Rupert can see that I need a minute.

"I'm going to go and ask if there is somewhere else we can use for art. Back soon."

When I'm alone, I look around the room and remember all the hope I felt yesterday when I walked in. How different I feel in here to the rest of the school. Rupert's right, it's not fair. I'm sick of being told what I can and can't do. For maybe the first time in my life I made a decision for myself and now they're taking it away from me. The tears vanish and turn into anger. A feeling like I have not felt before. I hear all the words from my parents last night, telling me who I should be. Telling me I'm not good enough. I picture the maths teacher tearing out my doodle. I look at the string of pictures heaped in an unloved pile. *It's not fair!* I think again, the rage still building. My breathing quickens and I feel like I'm about to explode. I need to do something. I need to show them that it's not OK to tell people who they should be. I need to show everyone that I won't listen any more. That I want to make my own decisions and I want my life to be mine.

I pick up a pot of paint and feel energy surging through me. I want to throw it across the room. I want to show them my anger. As I hold the paint in the air, ready to let go, a smaller voice in my head tells me to stop, to put the paint down and go and calm down. It tells me how cross Madeleine and John will be if I let go. But the rage is still there, that sharp sting of unfairness still real. I don't know what to do. Tears start streaming down my cheeks. Should I let go of the paint and show them who I am? Should I throw it? What would you do?

If you think I should **throw the paint**, turn to **page 207**.

If you think I should **put the paint down and leave the room**, turn to **page 185**.

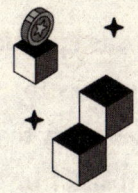

SIT WITH THE NAUGHTY KID

I'm about to walk towards Marco and sit where I know really that I should. I know it's the sensible decision but as I take a step in his direction, I see him lick his finger to turn the page of the book in his hands. He does it in just the same way that Madeleine does. An image immediately pops into my brain of her telling me what to do.

"Sit with Marco. Be polite. Why is he reading a book and you are not? Get a book, Fred. Be the best, Fred. Don't stand out."

I shake my head, trying to get rid of the image, but when it won't go, I change direction. I walk over to the chair dancer, who is now sitting with his legs sprawled out to the sides, arms lolling over the back of the chair.

"Hi, I'm Fred," I say, as I plonk myself next to him.

He looks at my trousers through narrowed eyes and so I cross my legs and try to cover them with my bag. Just as I'm about to ask him what his name is, he moves his chair so that he's kind of behind me. Then he gets his phone out and whispers, "Tell me if she's coming."

I look up at the teacher and Marco catches my eye. He looks quickly down at his book and I feel a twinge of guilt for not sitting with him.

I turn in my chair and see the chair dancer's scrolling through YouTube videos. His name tag is almost illegible, but I can make out the first name: *Jared*.

When he catches me looking at him, he hisses, "Keep watch, Frederick!" I turn quickly back to the front.

Our form teacher Mrs Machen takes the register and then tells us that this will be the seating plan for the first week.

"Sit in these positions for all your lessons, please, until you are told otherwise. Your first lesson is French and you can make your way there when the bell goes."

"Why are you wearing an apron, miss?" Jared's voice pipes up from behind me.

"I'm the food tech teacher," she says.

"Are you about to cook something, miss?" he asks. He sounds sincere but I can tell that he's messing with her.

"Not right now, no," she says, clearly wanting to shut down this line of questioning.

"Do you wear an apron all the time, miss?"

"Yes."

"Even at home, miss?"

A few people smirk and giggle. He asks the questions so confidently, as though he's actually interested. The teacher has no other option but to answer them.

"Not all the time at home, no."

"What about in bed, miss?"

"That's enough, thank you … Jared," she says, as she comes over and squints at his name badge, clearly making an internal note that he is trouble. Then the bell rings and we all stand up. Jared gets his phone back out and swaggers out of the classroom.

"No phones inside the school, please," Mrs Machen calls after him and he raises his thumb above his head as he passes her, clearly not putting the phone away. I follow him down the corridor. Part of me thinks being stuck with him is a terrible idea. That

I should ask to be moved immediately. But part of me is amazed by his confidence. Imagine speaking to a teacher like that – to anyone. He just doesn't care.

For the rest of the morning, I'm mesmerized by Jared's naughtiness. He throws stuff in French and then starts making fart sounds in science. In maths he asks the teacher so many questions about themselves that we barely do any actual maths. By lunchtime I can't help myself but laugh along with whatever he does to either get us all out of lessons or to entertain himself.

As we are packing our stuff up before lunch a lady comes in with a note and passes it to the teacher. He reads it.

"Fred Timple?" I look up, startled. Is this it? I've been caught already. Before I could even get to the art room, the whole reason I came here.

"Go to the school office when the bell goes, please," the teacher says, placing the note on the desk. I nod. She leaves the room and I sigh. It's over. I feel Jared's eyes on me.

"What did you do?" he says in a sing-song voice.

"Nothing," I say, but I feel my face getting redder.

"Don't believe you. If you tell me what it is I can get you out of it. I'm a master."

"It's—" I wonder if I should tell him. Maybe he can help me. But then I think about how loud and wild he is and decide against it.

"Nothing," I say.

"Whatever you say, Frederick," he says, and then as the bell goes he adds, "But if it were me, the last place I would be going right now is to the school office. By the look on your face, you want to avoid that for as long as possible. Am I right?"

I kind of nod without nodding and he laughs.

"I knew it! Just don't go, Fred. Say you forgot. When they come for you again, hide. The bogs is the best. I've got your back. I'll help. Now go, feed your face and then hide."

I do exactly what he says. I dash to the lunch hall, quickly realizing that I have no money or account or anything for this school. The Gains School uses thumbprints but that won't work here. I will have to let my tummy rumble. I add it to the growing list in my head of what I need to do for tomorrow.

Better trousers
A T-shirt
Wash the mushroom jumper
A packed lunch

All these things I need to keep totally hidden from Madeleine, which is easier said than done. She won't let me near the washing machine and I don't know how I will sneak a packed lunch out without her noticing.

I walk away from the lunch hall feeling my tummy gurgle at the smell of chips and head straight to the art block. If I can't eat food, at least I can draw some! I picture a huge bowl of spaghetti with strands coming out of the bowl, each wrapped around a thing on my list. I run towards the art room, through the outdoor corridor, looking up at all the murals and graffiti. When I walk into the classroom and see kids dotted about, painting or sculpting, I smile to myself. This is why I'm here. It will be totally worth all the lies, and Jared was right, whenever they come for me, I can just hide.

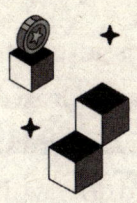

JARED

In the afternoon, halfway through geography, a teacher knocks on the door and peers in through the glass. I instantly know that she's coming for me and so does Jared. He shoves my head down under the desk and whispers, "Stay down, I've got you covered."

With my body crushed into a ball under the desk I can hear some muffled conversation from the front of the room and then I hear my name being called. I look up through the gap between the chair and the chewing-gum-filled desk bottom and see a snippet of Jared's face looking innocently back at the teacher.

"He's gone to the toilet, sir. He didn't feel well, sir. Shall I go and find him, sir?"

Then there is some more muffled talking and the teacher speaks more loudly.

"Tell him he needs to go straight to the school office when he gets back, please."

"Will do, sir," he says with a salute. I'm not exactly sure what I'm meant to do now. I can't stay down here for the whole lesson.

After five minutes, Jared whispers, "Come up." He grabs my jumper and drags me out.

"He'll see me," I whisper.

"He doesn't know who anyone is," he says, grinning. "Look at him, he doesn't even know what day it is."

I look at the teacher at the front. He has his glasses on his head and is patting his pockets and looking on the desk for the missing specs. I smile. Jared's right, he hasn't even noticed that I've popped back up.

By the end of the day, I'm exhausted. Waiting to be caught and figuring out various lies is pretty tiring. When I queue up for the bus and remember that I don't have a bus pass, I slap my hand to my forehead and groan. Jared appears by my side.

"What's the matter now, Frederick?"

"I don't have a bus pass and he won't let me on."

"Say no more. Watch and learn."

He gets on the bus and shows his pass and, as he asks the driver some ridiculous question about bus routes, I see his hand appear behind his back, holding out his pass for me to grab. I look around quickly to check that no one is watching and then snatch it. Jared swaggers off up the bus and I flash the pass, trying not to look too suspicious.

When I sit down next to Jared I hold out the pass and he shakes his head.

"Why don't you keep it?" he says, snapping photos of the pass with his phone.

"What about you?"

"My brother makes fake IDs, he can fake me one tonight."

"Are you sure?"

He nods and starts playing a game on his phone. He's really kind and slightly terrifying at the same time. How is he so good at getting away with things? And who has a brother that makes fake IDs?!

When I stand to get off the bus, he stands too. I know he didn't get on at my bus stop this morning, no one did, so I'm not sure why he is getting off here. But he follows me down the aisle and shouts to the driver, "Ta, big fella."

The driver laughs and shakes his head.

"Do you live round here?" I ask, as we stand at the bus stop.

"No." He grins. "That's not even my bus. I live over the other side of town. Do you want to go and find an empty building?"

"What?" I say.

"Follow me."

He heads off down the road towards the beach. I follow, as I'm not really sure what else to do and somehow I feel responsible for him being here at all. When we get to a long row of houses on the seafront, he heads to one with a *For Sale* sign by the gate and peers through the windows.

"No, they're still there," he says, almost to himself.

"What are we doing?" I whisper.

"Looking for a den," he says and runs to the next sign. I'm definitely starting to regret sitting with Jared.

After peering into the windows of four or five different houses all up for sale, he seems to find what he's looking for.

"Bingo," he says and walks through the gate and round to the back of the house. I know now that I shouldn't follow. I don't want to be here or do any of this, but he has helped me out all day. If it weren't for him I would have probably crumbled and told the teachers everything. Madeleine and John would have been called and they would be furious. I couldn't even have got home without him. I'm not sure what to do, so when I hear him call "Frederick?" I glance around and then follow the voice.

I get to the back yard and I can see his bum sticking out of a cat flap and hear the sound of his voice coming from inside the empty house.

"I'm too big. But there's a window up there we could get through."

No! I think. *I don't want to get through a window. I don't want to be here. This is totally illegal!* I look around frantically, trying to figure out what to do. My eyes land on a small shed. I try the door and it's open. Inside is a broken-looking, rusty lawnmower and some tins of paint.

"I've got it!" I shout and I see his head pop out of the cat flap and turn to me. He stands up and dusts himself off and comes over to the tiny shed. I smile and open the door for him.

"It's a den," I say when I see the unimpressed look on his face.

"It's not exactly living the high life, is it?"

"Why do you want a den anyway?" I ask.

"It's just fun finding places to hide out. Empty houses are cool."

"Won't your parents be worried?" I say, suddenly realizing that Madeleine will be wondering where I am.

"They don't care," he says.

"Look, I've got to go," I say, checking my watch and knowing that I'll have to run. "But thanks for everything. For the bus pass and helping me hide and stuff."

As I walk away, I see him get out a vape and blow a cloud of smoke my way.

"I've got your back, Frederick. I don't know what trouble you're in, but I've got you. If you've got me?"

"Yeah, sure," I say, wondering as I walk up the front path if I will regret those words.

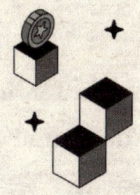

THE FIRE DECISION

I try to use the avoidance plan from school on Madeleine and John. I figure if I can get away with it on teachers then it might work at home. I scuttle up to my bedroom and when it's time for tea I call down that I'm not feeling hungry. Madeleine appears almost instantly at my door. I have sprayed the mushroom-smelling jumper with some of John's deodorant and shoved it under my bed but a strange smell is now filling my room and Madeleine scrunches her nose up.

"I've got a funny tummy," I say, trying to look sad and apologetic.

"Oh dear. I will bring you some food up in case you get hungry. How was your first day? I haven't even seen you."

"It was good," I say.

"Well, I hope you will be OK for tomorrow. It's not a good impression to take time off in the first week. Shall I call the head teacher?"

"NO!" I say too loudly and quickly, suddenly realizing that the Gains School will be wondering where I was today. I'm amazed they haven't already been on the phone and ruined it all. I need to make a plan.

I look at Madeleine and hold my tummy.

"You might want to get out of here before I make another smell," I say. She scrunches her nose again and closes the door. Bad smells are like Madeleine's nemesis.

When I can hear the pots and pans clinking in the kitchen, I know that I need to act fast. I sneak into John's office and lean over the desktop. Luckily he's always logged into his email account. I just need to email the school from his address and everything will be OK. I'm not sure how I made this cunning plan so easily. Maybe Jared's naughtiness is rubbing off on me.

When I get to the mailbox screen I search THE GAINS and an email pops up from the head teacher. Perfect. I click reply and I start typing.

Dear Mr Sourden,

My son Fred Timple was due to start at the Gains this week, but due to a last-minute change of plan he will not be joining the school.

I try to come up with a reason, another house move, maybe, or an illness, but then I remember something I saw on YouTube about lying that said it's best not to be specific. Say as little as you can. I try to put myself in the mind of John. To imagine what he would say. *I don't need to explain myself. I'm John Timple, for goodness' sake. I can send my kid to any school I like. I don't need to say anything to anyone.*

I carry on typing.

Yours sincerely,
John Timple

And then I can't help myself at the end, adding something else:

P.S. Do not contact me about this matter.
P.P.S. Your school is a bit scary.

I click *Send* and breathe a sigh of relief. That's the Gains sorted. I think of the other things on my list. My jumper smells weird but a bit less mushroomy. I sneak back to my room and pack some decent clothes in my bag to get changed into before I get to school tomorrow. I think that's everything. I'm feeling good.

My tummy rumbles and I decide that maybe I can cope with questions after all. I feel pretty invincible after the email and it's not like I can avoid my parents for ever. I run downstairs, missing every other step, and Madeleine and John look up from their shepherd's pie as they see me.

"Can you not leap down the stairs like that, please, Fred? I thought you had tummy ache?"

"Turns out I just needed a poo," I say, and sit down at the table.

"That is not how we talk at the dinner table, Fred! Honestly!" Madeleine looks horrified and John pats her arm.

"Your mother just wants some respect," he says. Then he takes a big drink and changes the subject.

"So, what teams did you sign up to, Fred?"

I delay my answer by shoving a huge forkful of shepherd's pie into my mouth, which gives me time to plan my response. They both watch me as my cheeks bulge with food and I make them wait until I have swallowed. By the time my mouth is empty I've still not thought of the right answer. I look around the room, desperately trying to think. My eyes land on a mug which is hanging on the mug tree. It has a boat on it.

"Sailing club," I say, immediately regretting it as I don't have the first clue about sailing. I shouldn't have picked something that I need to research.

"It's not what I would call a sport, but that's pretty impressive, Fred. I didn't even know they had a sailing team at the Gains."

"It's new," I say, the lies coming easily now.

Not wanting to take too many chances and tell too many lies, I shove the rest of my food into my mouth and take my plate to the dishwasher. I mumble something about homework and leave the kitchen, hearing Madeleine say "Delightful".

The next day I manage to change my clothes behind a bush on the way to the bus stop. I get on with Jared's pass and have some stolen food for lunch in my bag. I feel like everything is perfect. When I get to form time, Jared's already there and the rest of the kids are staring at him as he rummages through the drawers by the ovens. Some of the girls are not impressed and are saying things like "We will go and tell" and "Miss will be so cross when she gets here".

When Jared finds what he's looking for he comes and sits at our desk. I smile at him and he shows me a packet of matches from his pocket.

"What are you doing?" I say, horrified.

"If we set the fire alarm off, we get at least an hour off, I reckon."

Then he starts burning bits of paper from his bag. I stand up. I know that this is really bad. I have to stop him.

"Jared, stop it!" I say.

"Or what?" he says, grinning at me. "You'll tell the teachers? The ones you are hiding from?"

He holds an unlit match against the lighting strip on the side of the packet and flicks it towards me. The match lights as it starts to fly through the air, and I manage to jump out of the way. The match fizzles out on the floor, leaving a black mark. This doesn't feel good any more. It doesn't feel funny, like when he asks the teachers silly questions, this is properly dangerous. I'm praying that the teacher gets here now and stops him, but when I turn round Jared is burning a piece of cardboard and is waving it up towards the smoke detectors.

Smoke starts filling the room, and a few girls run out, saying they are going to tell. I see Marco coughing loudly as the rest of the room starts emptying. He's holding his jumper over his face.

"Get out, Marco!" I call, trying to put the fire out by wafting my folder behind Jared, but it just makes it worse. Marco doesn't move and keeps coughing. Even Jared realizes that it's gone too far and tries to blow out the burning cardboard but it only makes it stronger and he drops it on the desk, which lights the book underneath it. As the fire starts to blaze and Marco sounds like he's choking, the fire alarm finally rings out. The remaining kids start screaming and running towards the door. The room completely empties, apart from Marco and Jared.

"I'd leave him if I were you," Jared says, moving towards the corridor. "You probably want to keep your head down, don't you?"

I start to follow Jared but when I get over to the door I turn back and look at Marco. The fire growing behind him. Then I hear footsteps in the corridor and as I step out I see Mrs Rumbelow heading down the hallway towards us.

"Go now!" Jared says, as he turns to run. "They will look after the coughing kid. It's his own fault for not getting out. The smoke's not even that bad, I don't know why he's coughing like that."

I want to do as he says, to run and go and blend in with everyone in the yard. To get away with being here for another day. But I need to know that Marco is OK. I know that I should have stuck with him now. I take a step towards Marco and I know that if I carry on it's over. I will be caught and this is it. I will never wear this jumper again and I will never see that art room again. Mrs Rumbelow is heading my way, looking frantic. I don't know what to do. What would you do?

If you think I should **call for help for Marco and give myself up**, turn to **page 249**.

If you think that **Marco will be fine and I should run away**, turn to **page 227**.

office, frantically going through all the options in my brain. When I get there, I'm no closer to deciding what on earth to say.

The office lady looks at me over her glasses, raises her eyebrows and waits for me to speak.

"I'm Fred Timple," I say, feeling like I am handing myself over to the police.

"Ah, hello, Fred!" she says with a smile. "We seem to be in a bit of bother with your information. I know you only recently applied to Browtree but I can't find your details. I will need a phone number for your parents, or whoever is at home, so that I can contact them and get everything filled in. Is that OK?"

As I nod, a plan lands in my brain. I've got it!

"No problem," I say, trying not to grin and look too pleased with myself. "My mother's number is—" And then I smoothly recite my own phone number to the lady as she copies down every digit. She smiles at me.

"Aren't you good, knowing your mum's number off by heart? I will give her a call and sort everything out, nothing more for you to do, sweetie. Enjoy the rest of your first day!"

"I will!" I say, and then as I turn and walk away, I add, "She can be quite hard to get in touch with. She works very long hours."

"Oh, don't worry, sweetie, I'll leave her a message and she can call me back when she's free."

The second I'm out of the office I sprint to the toilets and take out my phone. I go to voicemail settings and delete the voice message of me saying "Leave a message, peeps". Instead I set it to a boring pre-recorded message that could be for anyone.

I've bought myself some time. Maybe not long, but at least I can stay here for now. I can go to the art room and then figure out what to do next.

When I get there Marco is already sitting at a table on his own, looking completely out of place. There are older kids spray-painting tags on to a huge white sheet, a girl with pink hair is doing some charcoal drawing and a few kids are dotted about with sketch pads. Marco is sitting there with a sandwich and his cube.

"You don't fancy working on a masterpiece?" I ask, as I sit down and start looking at all the paints and pastels.

"Not my thing." He frowns.

"What is your thing?" I ask, as I spread out a sheet of paper in front of me and feel the calm wash over me.

"I don't really have a thing," he says. "Apart from this."

He points at the cube and then keeps clicking it around.

I take a pencil and start sketching out an idea. A playground full of colourful robot children. One of them is in black and white, trying desperately to hide.

"You must be super brainy, though?" I say, as I draw.

"No." He sighs. "This is the only thing I'm good at. I learned it off YouTube. Anyone could do it."

"I couldn't," I say. "Anyway, you know loads of big words and you were reading a textbook in form time! You must be a right brainbox."

Marco looks up from his cube and then awkwardly down to the floor.

"I wasn't really reading the book and anyone can say a few big words. It's kind of not real. It's just a show."

"What do you mean?"

"I don't want to be some ordinary thick kid, so I pretend I'm not. People really believe it too, until they see my test results."

"Wow," I say.

"My dad says I'm a thicko masquerading as a boffin."

"Oh," I say, not really knowing what to say to

this. It sounds like a horrible thing for a dad to say. I'm suddenly really sad for Marco. He's not the kid I thought he was at all. But I'm not really sure now who he is. I just carry on with my drawing and Marco carries on clicking away at his cube.

Time seems to vanish, like it does when I'm drawing, and when the bell rings I can't believe I've been in here all lunch. I haven't even eaten anything, but I don't care. I'm so happy to be here. I'm even happy to be next to Marco. Maybe we're all just pretending to be someone we're not. But for the first time in my life I feel like maybe I am actually being the real version of myself. I feel like maybe I have been making the right decisions for once.

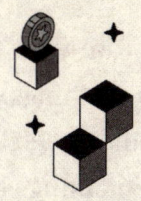

MAISIE MARVEL

After school I realize that I forgot to get a bus pass, and before I can run back to the office to get one my bus is pulling out of the bay. I see Marco walking down the road towards the shops.

"Marco!" I call, taking out my phone. I look up how long it will take me to walk home, and jog after Marco. "Wait up. I'm walking that way."

He slows down and lets me catch up. I see on my phone screen that it will take me half an hour if I walk fast. Hopefully Madeleine won't notice that I'm late. She doesn't know yet what time the Gains bus gets back anyway. I've also got to find somewhere to get changed and then come up with some first-day-at-the-Gains-School facts, so I can pretend that's where I have been all day.

"What's going on with you?" Marco asks, as my mind thinks of a million things.

I wonder if I should lie. Tell him that I'm not feeling well or that something else is wrong. I scroll through the options but I feel tired by all the lying. I look at Marco and decide that he seems pretty trustworthy.

"Can I tell you a secret?" I ask.

"Yeah, if you want to," Marco says matter-of-factly.

"But will you promise not to tell anyone?"

"Of course, Fred. That's kind of the definition of a secret."

He looks at me as though I'm dim, and I can't quite believe that he's not as intelligent as he seems. His dad must be wrong.

"I'm not really meant to be at Browtree," I say.

He narrows his eyes and tilts his head at me as we walk and I tell him everything. I tell him about how scary the Gains School was and how I found the jumper in the bush. I tell him about my lie to the receptionist and that I have no idea how to keep it all up.

"OK," he says, as he takes it all in.

"I want to stay at Browtree so much. I don't know what to do." I sigh and my shoulders slump.

"We can definitely fix this," he says.

"How?" I ask.

"We need to find someone to pose as your mum and I know just the person. Come with me."

He speeds up and I try to keep up. I quickly text Madeleine saying that the bus is late. At least that will buy me some time.

When we get to the chippy on the main road Marco knocks on a door with peeling black paint on it and a broken letter box.

"Where are we going?" I ask. "Is this where you live?"

"No, my sister Maisie lives here. She's eighteen. She can pretend to be your mum." I instantly think this is a bad idea. This feels like a bigger lie than the rest somehow. Surely eighteen-year-olds still sound like kids? But before I can say anything the door opens and a plume of vape smoke pours out. When the smoke clears, a girl with thick dark eyebrows that look like painted slugs smiles at us.

"What you want, squirt?" she asks and then turns and walks up the stairs to a tiny room with a bed and what looks like an explosion of make-up on every available surface. Marco follows her into the tiny room, babbling an edited version of the story that I told him.

"So, we need you to call school and leave a message. No one will be there now, so it'll go straight to voicemail. Pretend to be his mum. Tell them he is meant to be there and you will send all the paperwork they need through the post as you are too busy to come in."

"OK, kiddo," she says, as if this is the most normal thing in the world. Before I can say a single word, she is on the phone.

"What's her name?" she whispers.

"Madeleine Timple," I say.

"And yours?"

"Fred."

When she starts it's like watching an Oscar-winning actress. She's mesmerizing. By the end of the message, I almost believe that she is my mum.

"What about the other school?" she says when she's finished the call.

"The Gains? What about it?" I ask.

"Won't they wonder where you are?"

I'd not even thought about that. I was so busy trying to get away with being at Browtree I forgot that my name would still be down at the Gains. My face goes pale, but before I can worry too much, she is on the phone again, leaving a message at the Gains saying that I have diarrhoea and won't be in for the rest of the week. She really is incredible.

"If you say you've got the squits no one will be chasing you down for a while. Not sure what you will do next week but you will have to figure that one out. Right, off you go, kiddo, I've got to go and shovel fish in ten minutes."

As we walk down the stairs she ruffles Marco's hair.

"How was the first day? Learn any more big, fancy words?"

Marco swats her hand away and goes red.

"How is it at home this week, kiddo?" she asks.

"Same." Marco sighs. He looks different for a second. Scared and sad.

"Not long and I will get you out of there, I promise," she says gently.

He nods and I feel a pang of worry and confusion.

"What does she mean?" I ask when we get out on to the road.

He stops and looks at me seriously.

"Can I tell you a secret?" he asks, and for a moment I'm not sure that I want him to.

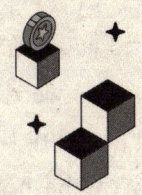

THE SECRET

Back at home, and back in my Gains blazer, I tell Madeleine that I'm desperate for the loo and then run straight upstairs and lock myself in the toilet. I put the lid down and sit on top, putting my head in my hands, pressing my fingers into my scalp as though I might be able to push all the things Marco told me out of my head.

I thought my house was strange and my parents were controlling, but what Marco said made me think that maybe my life is pretty good. Even though I can't paint or make a mess or put my art on the walls. Maybe knowing what meal you're having every day is actually a good thing. Marco has to cook for himself most nights and that's if there is even any food in the cupboards.

At first, I thought he was just moaning, like most kids do, saying his parents were awful and that they don't really care about him, but then he said that they leave him. Leave him in the house for days. That's when I knew that this wasn't just normal kid stuff. I can't get the look on his face out of my head when he told me. His words running over and over in my head.

"I don't make a fuss," he said. "Otherwise my dad gets REALLY angry."

His sister is trying to earn enough money for a flat so that they can run away and he can live with her. They've got an escape plan. That's the secret.

It feels too much. Too grown-up a problem for me to deal with. My mind is racing. How will his sister get a bigger flat? Will he even be allowed to live with her anyway? He can't be left alone in the house again – what if something happened to him?

I know this is bad. I know that I should tell someone, but I also know that I made a promise. He's keeping my school secret and so surely I have to keep his? Anyway, who would I tell? I can't tell Madeleine or John and I can't tell anyone at school. My cover would be instantly blown and surely Marco needs me at Browtree now that I know.

Maybe I can help him without having to tell

anyone. Then I start to question how bad it even is. Maybe kids are left on their own all the time. Just because my parents won't even go to the shop without me, in case I "set the place on fire", doesn't mean other parents are the same. Maybe I need to find out. I do an unnecessary flush and go downstairs.

I manage to get through the first-day-at-school questions pretty well and by the time tea is on the table I'm actually enjoying telling made-up stories about the Gains School. I have invented some teachers who John says remind him of teachers from when he was there. I tell them that I have joined the rugby team and the football team, which they are ridiculously thrilled by. It's almost easier, being the version of the child they want me to be.

As I'm finishing up my shepherd's pie, I slip in a question.

"Is it illegal for an eleven-year-old to be in the house on their own?" I ask as casually as I can.

"Why, Fred? You planning on getting rid of us?" John says, laughing.

"No, I just heard some kids talking on the bus and I wondered."

"Well, I don't think it's illegal, not if it's just for a bit, but I would say it is unwise."

"What if they were on their own for days?" I ask innocently.

"Well, that's another story, Fred. Yes, that would be a problem for the social services or the police."

"Did these boys say that as well, Fred?" Madeleine asks, clearly worried now.

"No, not at all. I just wondered, that's all."

"You let us know if you hear any more of that kind of talk and I will be on the phone to the school."

"Yes, I will," I say, biting the inside of my lip.

I take my plate and make my excuses, saying that I have homework. Then I head upstairs and message Marco:

> I've been thinking about what you told me. Do u think u should tell someone at school?

His reply is instant:

> Of course I don't. That would make my life worse than it is. If u tell anyone I will tell about u.

> We made a promise.

I breathe in and out slowly. This is bad. Really bad. There's a knock at the door and Madeleine puts her head round, looking into the bedroom.

"Are you OK, Fred?" she asks.

I nod and try to smile. She steps into the room.

"They were very specific questions you were asking at teatime. You know you can tell me anything, don't you?"

"Yeah," I say, feeling like I might cry or blurt it all out at once.

"Do you think someone might be in trouble?" she asks. When I don't say anything, she adds, "I can call the school and let them know, sweetie, it's no problem."

I need to make a decision, right now. I can breeze over it as though everything is OK and tell her some lads were chatting about a film they had seen about a kid in the house on their own, say it just made me wonder and that there is nothing at all to worry about.

Or I can tell her.

I can try to find a way of telling her and not giving away my secret too. I could tell her that I met Marco at the bus stop. That he's not at my school. I could just tell her his name and she could call whoever she needs to call. She doesn't need to even know he goes to Browtree. Maybe he won't even know that I have told anyone. I might still get away with all of it, but Marco would be safe. The social workers or police or whoever can check out his house and make sure everything is OK.

But of course he would know it was me. I just sent that stupid text message. After what he has done to help me, that would be awful. He would feel betrayed.

I look up at Madeleine's face waiting for an answer. I don't know what to do. What would you do?

If you think I should **tell Madeleine about Marco**, turn to **page 289**.

If you think I should **keep Marco's secret**, turn to **page 267**.

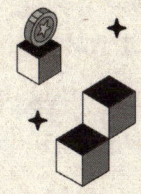

STAND UP TO THE BULLIES

As I alternate looks between Callum and Rupert, I see the blood soak through the tissue that Rupert's holding to his nose. It's dripping on to his PE shirt. He needs me to help him. I can't just leave him, can I? Even if it means not being the kind of kid who would make John proud. Maybe I don't want to be that kid anyway.

"You need more tissue," I say to Rupert and start to walk past Callum towards the toilet.

"What are you doing?" Callum asks, holding me back.

"I'm helping my friend," I say clearly, looking right into his eyes, and then I push past him and hear him hoot with sinister laughter. When I get back with some toilet roll and hand it to Rupert, Callum is still there watching us.

"How romantic," he says, and the hunters all come and stand with him.

"Boys, look at this. Isn't it beautiful? Fred here had the option of hanging out with us and instead he chose to nurse his little girlfriend."

One of the boys whistles with his fingers and they all howl. When the bell goes and we realize that we're late, even the hunters look worried. They rush off to get ready and as they head out of the changing room, Callum turns back.

"I'd watch myself if I were you, Fred," he shouts. "If I bump into you in the hall, you might end up with a matching nosebleed."

I watch them leave and pull my uniform on quickly, as Rupert struggles to try and not get blood all over his shirt. When we eventually leave the changing room and Rupert's nose has finally calmed down, the bald coach is standing at the door.

She smiles and says, "Hurry up, boys, you will be late." Then she looks at me and adds, "Well done for looking after him."

Rupert looks at me as we rush down the corridor and smiles.

"Thanks, Fred."

"No worries. I wasn't about to ditch you for those bullies."

I know that, in another life, and on a different day, I might have made the total opposite decision.

"Well, I know it was tempting, so thanks. It makes it even kinder that you chose me. Not everyone would have," he says, as though he could sense my indecision.

We walk fast to the history room and as we walk in late and the teacher looks like he might explode at us, Rupert holds up the bloody tissue and the teacher sighs and tells us to sit down quickly.

As I sit down and open my book, I can feel my heart beating in my chest. It calms and slows as I breathe and I know that I've done the right thing. I've made the right choice, I'm sure of it.

After school as we're walking towards the bus bay Rupert thanks me again and asks if I want to go to his house.

"I think Madeleine would literally explode if I rang and asked her two days in a row!" I smile. "Shall I ask her if I can come tomorrow? Maybe stay and sample Jessie's cooking this time?"

"Yeah," he says, smiling. "That would be great."

When I get home, I immediately know that something is wrong. It's like the air in the house is full of rage and tension. It's quiet. No sound of cleaning or cooking. I want to turn round and go straight to my spot on the beach, but I know I need to go further into the house. To see if what I am sensing in the atmosphere is real.

When I have silently removed my shoes and put them away, I look into the empty kitchen and wonder where Madeleine is. The door wasn't locked so she's in here somewhere. It feels like a horror movie, like I'm waiting for something or someone to jump out at me and make me scream. When I have looked downstairs and can feel myself getting more and more panicky, I change my pace and dash up the stairs. When I see my bedroom door open, I instantly know what is going on. She's in my bedroom. She has found the mess I made yesterday and has seen the pictures all over the walls.

When I left this morning, I was so happy to wake up and see my paintings and drawings all over the walls. I was even happy with the clothes all over the floor. A part of me knew that I should put it all away. That I should hide my artwork again, but I told myself that she wouldn't go in. I thought it could be my secret. Just for a couple of days, I could have the bedroom that I wanted. With everything happening with Rupert and the hunters I didn't even think about it.

When I walk into my room, she's sitting on the bed surrounded by my art. She's silently sobbing, and when she sees me she wails, "Get out! Get out of this house."

I want to say something, to make it OK, but no words come out and so I turn and run. Downstairs. Shoes on and out where I wanted to be anyway. To my spot on the beach where I can be free to be me.

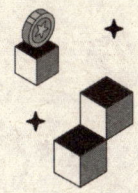

EVERYTHING FORGOTTEN

I want to stay on the beach all night but I know that if I don't get home for tea then everything will be worse, so I reluctantly dust the sand off my bum and trudge back to the house. I can't get the sound of Madeleine's voice out of my head. It sounded like she was in physical pain. Sometimes I think mess and clutter actually hurt her somehow.

I have no idea what to expect when I get home. She will have shown John and he will mostly be annoyed by all the art. I think about the pictures they will have seen. The robot versions of them both. Thinly veiled, cartoonish stories of how controlled I feel by them. He will be fuming as well.

So, when I get in and see them both calmly sitting

at the dining table waiting for me, the tea spread out in front of them, I pause. What are they doing? Why is Madeleine not crying any more? John looks completely normal.

"Go and get changed out of your uniform, Fred, please. You really shouldn't go to the beach in it. You have ten minutes until tea."

Madeleine's voice sounds no tighter than usual. Her tone is even slightly bright. I walk slowly upstairs, wondering what will be there when I open the door to my room.

I slowly step towards the closed door, scared but not even imagining what could be on the other side. I stand still for a few moments and then give the door a nudge. I peer through the gap and it looks like it always does. The bed is made. The clothes are gone, and when I look at the walls, all I see are boats. I run into the lifeless room and search for my pictures. I look in every drawer and cupboard but they're gone.

I know what she has done. She has erased it. It's as if the whole thing never happened. I bet she didn't even tell John. She couldn't cope with how it made her feel, so she's pretending it didn't happen.

I feel confused. Like I should be grateful. She's not cross any more. I've got away with it. But for some reason I don't feel grateful or relieved or happy. I feel invisible. All my art has been taken.

When I go downstairs to eat the same sausage and chips and broccoli that we have every Wednesday and answer the same questions about school and listen to the same chat about weather and work, I feel something building inside my chest. It feels like a bubble of something solid, dark and angry. It feels like if it doesn't come out, I might scream or pass out.

As they discuss what they're going to watch on telly, I know that I need to do something. My chips are getting stuck in my throat and I can feel tears in my eyes. I want her to say something. I want her to shout at me or mention my pictures. A tiny part of me wants her to acknowledge that I'm actually good. I know that she never will. I have to do or say something before my sausage and chips burst out of my mouth and I scream until my throat is sore. I can feel the anger building but when the words finally come, they are tiny and quiet.

"What did you do to my room?" I ask.

Madeleine ignores me and pours some water from the jug.

"Hurry up, Fred, you are taking an age."

"What did you do to my room?" I say again, a little bit louder this time.

I see her pause slightly and give a tiny shake of her head. Then she smiles a fake smile and starts clearing the table.

"I don't know what you are talking about, Fred. Eat up."

She turns away from the table to the sink. John then finishes his last chip and takes his plate and joins her. Their backs facing me as the tears leak out of the corners of my eyes. I angrily wipe them away and scrape my sausages into the bin before running from the room back to my cold, sterile bedroom.

As I fling myself on the bed, I see my phone light up. It's a message from Rupert:

> Did you ask your mum about tomorrow? Jessie is making risotto.

I type back before I can overthink what to say and hit *Send*.

> My mum just threw away every single piece of art that I ever made and is now pretending it never happened.

I see that he is typing. Then stopping then typing again. I wonder if I've said too much. Then his answer pops up:

> Wow. I'm sorry. Why would she do that?

I type back:

> She hates art. It feels like she hates me too.

> You need to talk to her.

> She won't listen. They never do.

> Maybe you need to try harder to be heard.

I look at the phone and think about what he has said. Have I tried hard enough? My voice at teatime was so small. I barely said anything, even though the feeling inside was so strong. But the way they make me feel is so suffocating, like I don't have the words to tell them anything. To say anything real about who I am or what I really want. I can't remember the last time that I actually said no to something or told them about how I felt or what I wanted.

I type back to Rupert:

> Maybe. I'm not really sure how.

The tears leak out of my eyes again as I hit *Send*. I feel lost. Another message pops up:

> Start with the truth. I will help. I may not be good on a basketball court but if my family is good at anything it's talking about our feelings!

> See if you can come for tea tomorrow and we can make a plan.

I smile and send a thumbs up. Then I start to worry about asking Madeleine if I can go out for tea. She will huff and make me feel guilty. She will talk about the meal plan and John will say I should be at home working or doing something more productive.

Maybe I can play them at their own game. If she's pretending that nothing is wrong, then I can too. I can lie and pretend that everything is fine. I wipe my eyes and go back downstairs. They're both sitting in front of the TV and I take a confident step into the room.

"My new friend Rupert has asked me to go to his house for tea tomorrow."

There's a pause and I feel Madeleine tense up, so I turn my attention to John. I know just what to say to get him on board.

"He's on the basketball team with me and his brother is a cyclist, almost professional."

Then, as I see his impressed look, I turn back to Madeleine.

"I wanted to give you plenty of warning, so I didn't land you in it tomorrow."

Then I smile a fake smile and tilt my head as if the decision has already been made.

"Fine," Madeleine says, barely hiding her annoyance.

"Sounds good, kid," John says. "I knew the Gains was the right place for you."

Then they both go back to watching their programme and I turn and go back upstairs. Maybe shoving all my feelings down and being just like them is not such a bad thing after all.

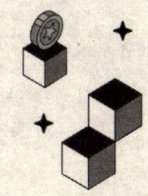

THE FIGHT

"Are you OK?" Rupert asks, as I walk through the huge iron school gates. It looks like he's been waiting for me and when I see him standing there, I feel the prickle of tears in my eyes. I shake them off and ignore whatever feelings are trying to escape out of my eyeballs.

"Yeah, I'm fine," I say. "Everything's sorted. I can come over tonight."

"Great. We can figure out a way for you to talk to your folks. They need to know how important art is to you."

"I've decided to just keep it hidden," I say, feeling the familiar prickle in my eyes again. "They don't get it. There's no point, so I will just pretend to be the kid they really want."

"I'm not sure that's a good—"

But before he can finish, the bell goes and I walk off quickly before he has a chance to make me question anything.

"Come on!" I shout. "It's robotics today. Maybe all the science nerds will pick on me and you will need to stick up for *me* this time!"

I turn back and he laughs but he looks sad. I realize that I have cut him off from speaking in the same way that my parents do. By ignoring the truth of what he was saying and glossing over it, I'm doing the thing I hate so much. Maybe it's inevitable. Maybe we all end up like our parents sooner or later.

By the time we get to lunch, Rupert has given up asking me if I'm OK. We head to robotics and his face seems to light up when we walk into the science room. It's filled with wires and batteries and things I don't even recognize. He sits down at a computer and pulls a chair out for me.

"I'm just going to the loo," I say, dumping my bag. "You get started."

As I walk down the corridor to the toilet block, I see Callum and his mates up ahead. I half consider turning round and going to the toilets over by the PE hall but they've already seen me.

"Where's your girlfriend, Fred?"

I carry on as if I haven't heard them, and walk into the toilets. I go into a cubicle and can feel my heart start racing. This was not a good idea. I'm now trapped in here. I look under the cubicle to see if there are any other feet. To see if there is any kind of protection from them if they come in. It's too late. I hear the door swing open and I jump up. I stand in the cubicle; the need to wee has vanished. I hear Callum's voice calling my name in a sing-song tone.

"Fred."

I hear him push a door open so hard that it swings and hits the wall.

"Freddy."

Another door smashes open. I can feel my heart almost bursting from my chest. I think of all the ways I could get out of this. I could go out and tell them that I really hate hanging out with Rupert, that they are way cooler and I would much rather be their mate. I could tell them that they're amazing at basketball and that we could go and have a game now. I could tell them what they want to hear. Just like when I tell my parents exactly what they want to hear. As I think about all the lies and fake smiles, all the polite conversation and pretending, I feel the tears finally falling down my cheeks. All of this is happening because I chose to get on the bus and come to this horrible school. I chose to join a team that I didn't even want to be on, and now I'm terrified in a toilet and wondering how I can carry on pretending to be someone who I'm not. What choice do I have now? I can choose to be the kid John would want. To become mates with these bullies and to pick on kids like Rupert. Or I can fight back. I can choose to be me and fight for myself.

As I hear the next door slamming open, I feel a wave of fury fill my entire body. This isn't fair. I'm not doing this any more. I unlock the door and swing it open and stand in front of the gang of hunters. I can feel sweat dripping down my chest and my hands are shaking. This time, though, it's not fear. I am furious. I shove Callum out of the way and then stand and look him straight in the eye. He looks confused. He didn't expect me to come out. He thought he could scare me and control me. But I'm not going to let that happen.

"I didn't want to sit with you yesterday because you're a bully," I say. "You are cruel and laddy and pointless. You can scare loads of kids in this school but I'm not scared of you, Callum."

He is silent for a split second and then he laughs.

"You're not scared?"

He lunges towards me as if he is going to headbutt me, but I don't flinch.

"No, I'm not," I say, as I feel his hands grab me and he wrestles me to the ground.

His hands are now on my face and as we writhe around the floor I'm vaguely aware that a crowd is forming. Kids, sniffing out the drama of a fight, come and fill the toilets and peer in through the door. As his sharp elbow digs into my chest, making it hard to breathe, he is pulled off me and all of a sudden it's over. The crowd are hushed and I can feel buzzing pain in my head and ringing in my ears.

"Both of you, straight to Mr Sourden's office now, please," comes the angry voice of the teacher who is still holding a red-faced Callum.

Half an hour later, outside the head teacher's office, we're waiting for our parents to arrive. Mr Sourden called them and Callum instantly started crying. I'm sitting here and I feel nothing. I feel numb.

When they get here, they come rushing in and immediately start saying that it can't have been my fault. That I wouldn't hurt a fly. Mr Sourden sits us down and asks for my side of the story.

"He's horrible, sir," I say. "He's a bully." And then I pause and add, "But I did push him first."

Madeleine gasps and John just shakes his head. shakes his head. I carry on and tell them everything. When they run out of questions, John stands up as though it's all sorted.

"It's quite clear that my boy was only standing up for himself. Sometimes it's all these kids understand."

"I will speak to the other boy and his parents and let you know our decision. Go home now and think about what kind of future you want, young man."

In the car it's silent and I know that when we get home tea will be on the table at six, my room will have been hoovered yet again and we will pretend that nothing has happened. I can feel the angry feeling start to build again in my chest. I can't ignore it or shove it down any more.

"Stop the car," I shout from the back seat. "Stop the car!"

"What are you talking about, Fred? What on earth has got into you?"

"Pull over!" I scream.

John pulls the car into a lay-by and they both turn their confused, angry faces towards me.

I know this is it. I have to tell them how I feel.

But where do I start? It's not easy telling the truth. I don't even know what the truth is at this point But I know that if I don't try then I will live like this for ever. Shoving down feelings and then exploding. Pretending to be someone that I'm not.

"I hate sports teams," I say, tears falling again.

John frowns, so I look down at my knees and find more true things to say.

"I want to be an artist."

They don't speak and so I carry on.

"I love art more than anything else in the world. I'm good at it. Really good. I should be allowed to paint and draw and make a mess."

I look up and Madeleine is crying. I look down again.

"I can't be the kid that you want me to be and I'm sorry but I have to be me. I've been hiding myself away because I was scared of you. I was scared of making you stressed or angry or disappointed and I can't do it any more. I'm not scared any more."

"Fred!" John's voice sounds cross, but not as confident as it normally does. I carry on.

"I will work hard at school, I will be home on time and be tidy for you, Madeleine."

Then I stop myself.

"Mum," I say. "I will be tidy for you, Mum."

She looks at John in surprise.

"I want to call you Mum and Dad," I say. "I want to put my own pictures on my bedroom walls, and I want to feel like I can make decisions for myself. I know that it's a lot to take in, but that's what I want."

They stay in a shocked silence and then I add, "Now, I want to go to Rupert's house for tea, like I was meant to. He will be worried about me, and his sister has cooked tea for me. You can think about what I've said and I'll be home later. We can talk about it all then. We can figure it all out together. It's all going to be fine, it will just be a bit different – it has to be."

I open the car door and start walking. I'm half expecting them to chase after me, to shout and scream and tell me to get back in the car. But they don't. They sit and stare and watch me walk away with mouths wide open. I turn back and give them a smile, knowing that whatever happens next, whatever they say to me when I get home, I will be OK because I know what I want. I want to fight for myself and I know I can.

To find out what happens next, turn to **page 311**.

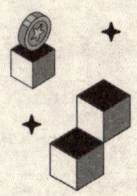

THE BALD LADY

I am so sick of making decisions based on what other people want me to do. Maybe I should start thinking about myself for a change. Maybe hanging out with these boys will be good for me. They could be a proper gang of mates, just like John wants me to have. We could become the best basketball team in the league and I could be the star player.

I picture myself scoring a winning basket and being held in the air by the hunters. Callum didn't mean to hurt Rupert anyway, did he? He was only messing about, and Rupert should have put his hands up. Maybe Rupert will be grateful. I can tell him that he doesn't have to come to basketball club after all. I will be fine. Maybe I've found the thing I'm good at. Maybe John was right. I might be even better at this than art.

I turn to Rupert, whose nose is still bleeding. He looks even smaller than usual.

"Maybe basketball is not the best club for you after all?" I say, taking a step towards Callum.

"You can say that again," he says quietly.

"Well, how about I hang with these guys and you get yourself sorted? You don't have to come again."

He looks up at me over his bright red tissue, which is now dripping on to his PE shirt. He smiles a sad smile and nods as if he knows exactly what this means.

"OK," he says. "Good idea."

Callum immediately grabs me by the shoulder and takes me over to where the hunters are getting changed. One of them has pinned down another one and is spraying deodorant in his face. The others are all laughing, even though it looks horrible. I laugh a fake laugh to join in and then have a quick glance back at Rupert who looks back and gives a half-smile.

"What other sports do you play, Fred?" Callum asks, as he takes his PE shirt off. He has muscles on his chest and looks more like a man than an eleven-year-old.

"I used to play rugby," I say. "But I'm not that into it."

I try to get changed without any of them seeing my skinny chest. I'm scared that one of them will pin me down and spray me with deodorant.

"Imagine his girlfriend playing rugby," one of the hunters says. He's the biggest of all of them and has a gold necklace on.

"What's his name?" Callum asks, pointing at Rupert.

"Rupert," I whisper. I want them to leave him alone. I try to think of a way to change the subject.

"What sports do you do?" I ask feebly.

"Rupert," Callum hoots. "You've got blood all over your face, Rupert. Do you want to call your mummy?"

They laugh again and I realize that they all laugh even when things aren't remotely funny. One of them starts singing "Rupert" over and over again. I watch as Rupert gets dressed and runs out of the changing room. I feel bad. I feel a little bit sick and like my tummy is not happy at all. But it might have been even worse if I had stayed with him. They might have gone for both of us. I'll talk to him later.

"What's with the bald lady coach?" the smallest and quietest of the hunters says. "She weirds me out."

"My brother said she had a nervous breakdown and all her hair fell out."

"Serves her right for being so mean," Callum says.

"I heard she shaves it off to look extra scary," the boy with the chain says.

"Well, it worked. She looks like a right horror show." Callum hoots.

I just get changed and say nothing. I don't know how to join in. It's almost like they can sense that I'm out of place. I'm being too quiet and they know it.

"What do you reckon, Fred? Why has old Baldy got no hair?"

I know that I can't say the truth. That it's probably because she's really sick and has had treatment that makes her hair fall out, like my auntie Sarah had. That won't make them hoot or laugh, will it? I try and think of something that will work. Something that will actually make me blend in with them. Something cruel or funny.

Then I have an idea for a drawing, and an image pops into my head. A robot version of the teacher putting a wig on her metal head. It's a horrible image and it makes me shiver, but it might do the job.

"Maybe she's not even human and that's why she can't grow hair. She's full of wires and metal and she's programmed to be mean," I say.

They all stop and look at me.

"That's weird," the boy with the chain says.

I don't think I've said the right thing. They're looking at me like I'm strange, but then Callum says, "Yeah, like RoboCop but RoboTeacher. Maybe she goes around the school killing students."

"Maybe she eats them," I add, getting into it a little bit now.

"Maybe she steals them and keeps them hostage in her weird house," adds the quiet hunter.

As we are all adding to the story and getting more and more carried away, there's a knock at the changing-room door.

"Out now, boys, get to your next lessons, please."

It's her voice. We all gasp and put our hands over our mouths.

"She's after us!" Callum says.

The bell rings and we all get our bags and walk through the door and past the bald PE teacher, unable to hide our snorts and giggles as we go. When I look back and catch her sad face, as she watches us walk away, I feel a horrible pang of guilt.

"We made it out alive, Fred," Callum says, putting his arm around my shoulder. "We live to see another day."

"Yeah." I smile, pretending to enjoy being part of

the gang, even though I'm seriously questioning if I made the right choice this time.

If I could rewind time and stay sitting with Rupert, would I? What if I can undo what I have done? Maybe I just need to say sorry and the next time it happens make the other choice. Make the choice to sit by his side. Maybe decisions aren't final. Surely I can change something if I feel like it was wrong?

What would you do? Would you go back and change things? Would you let the boys walk ahead, apologize to Rupert and next time you see them just say you made a mistake and that you are sticking by your new friend?

> If you want to **change your mind and stay with Rupert**, go back to **page 141** and change your decision.
>
> If you want to **stay with the hunters**, then **carry on reading**.

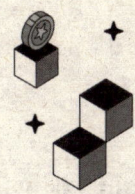

DRAWING THE POSTER

When I see Rupert in geography, he smiles at me awkwardly as I sit down.

"You don't have to sit next to me," he says.

"Don't be daft," I say. "Anyway, we don't have a choice for now, do we?"

I can still see crusty bits of dried blood around his nose and I want to tell him to wipe it off but it feels too weird, so we just sit in silence for the whole lesson and then, when the bell goes, he picks up his bag and turns to me.

"Don't bother about robotics club tomorrow."

"Oh, OK," I say, knowing that this would be the moment to say something, to do something different and change my path. I go to open my mouth but nothing comes out. I've made my choice to stick with the hunters so maybe it's for the best that I don't go to robotics anyway.

Rupert waits, as though he knows that this is the moment where I could change things, and when I don't, he shrugs his shoulders and packs up his pencil case.

"No offence, but I don't really need a friend like you."

I feel my neck getting hotter and the warmth travelling up my face.

"I hope you find whatever it is you are looking for with those boys," he says, and smiles a kind smile and then walks away.

I feel a whole mix-up of things. I'm annoyed and want to tell him to get lost. That he's just jealous that they don't want to hang out with him. I feel like a little kid who has just been told off and might burst into tears at any moment. Mostly I feel sorry, though. Sorry for Rupert but mainly sorry for myself. Sad and sorry that deep down I know that I'm missing out on being friends with someone as kind as Rupert. I try and push away the feeling and let the annoyed, angry feelings come to the surface instead, as I know what to do with them a bit more.

"Whatever, Rupert," I call after him, as I leave the

classroom. "I didn't want to come to the boring club anyway."

I watch his head bob down the corridor and he doesn't look back. Then I feel a slap on my back.

"Lovers' tiff?" Callum says with a grin.

"He's a loser," I huff.

"Too right, mate. He can't even catch a ball."

Then Callum gets out a piece of paper and unfolds it.

"Look what we made in RE."

CHILD-EATING TEACHER ON THE LOOSE. PROTECT YOUR CHILDREN!

"We just need a picture of old Baldylocks," he says, and before I can think long enough to stop myself, I say, "I can draw a picture."

"Awesome. We're going to photocopy it and put it in all the lockers."

"Won't we get into trouble?" I say.

"We won't get caught! Bring us a picture tomorrow."

I think about getting home and what I will draw, and an image of my trashed bedroom with all my pictures taped up on the walls flashes into my head. I didn't tidy it this morning. I kind of wanted Madeleine to find it but now that's the last thing I want. I've made friends with lads on a team and I'm good at basketball. I want Madeleine and John to see all that, not my destroyed bedroom. Madeleine will kill me. As soon as the bell goes for home time, I call her. She sounds normal enough when she answers.

"Have you been in my room yet today?" I ask.

"No. I'm literally on my way with some washing. Why?"

"Don't go in!" I say quickly. Then I add, "There's a surprise in there I don't want you to see."

"OK. You'll have to put all your clothes away as soon as you get in, then. I don't want them hanging around for days."

I smile. Of course she's more bothered about what to do with the washing than anything else.

"Leave it on the stairs and I'll do it when I get back," I say.

I open my sketchbook on the bus and hesitate before I start to draw the image of the robot teacher. This doesn't feel quite the same as my other drawings. It feels like I'm doing it for the wrong reasons. But what choice do I have? I told Callum I would do it. I volunteered. I sigh and put my pencil to the paper and let it move. By the time I get home the outline is done. There is no doubt who the drawing is of. Somehow even the robot version of her looks both angry and sad.

"How was basketball?" John says at tea, after I have put my room back to normal and all the washing is safely away.

"Yeah, I'm pretty decent actually," I say, smiling. After an afternoon of feeling horrible it feels nice to tell him that I'm good. To be honest and tell him what he wants to hear, knowing that everything is in its place upstairs and I'm not going to get into trouble. I carry on. After all, this is exactly what he wanted. I've made the decisions that he would want me to make, so maybe if I tell him, it will all be worth it.

"I made friends with a group of lads who are really good. I reckon the team could do pretty well. They are so tall! Wait till you see me, I actually scored loads of baskets!"

As I'm talking I feel better and better, as though I'm convincing myself that this was OK. That it was all meant to be.

"Callum is hilarious," I continue. "He's a bit cheeky but he's dead sporty and a right laugh.

Honestly, John, you should have seen me play. They all thought I was great."

I look up from my plate and smile at John, waiting for him to tell me how proud he is. How it sounds like I've done really well. When he speaks his tone is flat and not what I had hoped at all.

"Well, don't get too big for your boots, Fred, no one likes a show-off."

"Eat up," adds Madeleine.

We finish the rest of our tea in silence and I feel more alone than ever.

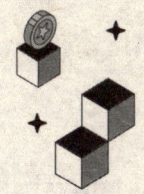

THE CONSEQUENCES

As soon as I get off the bus, I see Callum and the hunters standing by the gates.

"Freddo!" Callum calls. "Show us your artistic creation, then."

I finished the picture last night. It looks just like I'd imagined it in my head. The robot arms placing the wig wonkily on the bald metal head and scared children screaming in the background.

"I'm not sure we should show it to anyone," I say, as I hand it over.

"Whoa, this is sick!" Callum says, as he passes it to all the lads. They all hoot and gasp.

"You've got mad skills, Fred," the quiet hunter says.

"Everyone has to see this," says the one with the chain.

"But they'll know it's my drawing," I say.

"How?"

"Well, it's in my style."

"They don't even know what your style is, Fred, it's the first week! Anyway, we're only showing it to other kids."

They turn and walk off with my drawing and I know this is not going to end well, but I'm not sure there is anything I can do about it.

By lunchtime they've managed to photocopy the poster in the library without getting caught and have one hundred copies. They have made some alterations as well. Now the writing says:

SOME TEACHERS ARE TOO SCARY TO TEACH. I'D BE THAT ANGRY TOO IF I WAS BALD.

"That's a bit much," I say, knowing they won't listen. They are already folding the paper and posting it through the gaps in the lockers.

"We are going to be heroes." Callum grins. "Stunts like this go down in history."

"Don't you think it's a bit mean, though?" I ask. "What if she sees it?"

"She deserves it. She's horrible."

"I think she might be sick," I say, knowing that I should try and stop them but not really giving it my all.

"She's sick all right," Callum says, as he posts another poster into another locker.

I put my hands on my face and rub my eyes. I don't know what to do. I'm not quite sure how I ended up here. I follow them aimlessly for a few minutes and then stop and watch them disappear down the corridor of lockers.

After lunch I see a few people sniggering and holding the posters. I feel worse and worse every time I see one. I hope they all just go away and tomorrow it's forgotten about.

By the last lesson everyone is talking about the poster. Some people think it's hilarious, but I hear a group of girls saying how cruel it is. We sit at our desks for maths and Rupert looks at me and gives a tiny shake of his head. He knows.

"Why are you looking at me like that?" I hiss. He sighs and looks down at his book.

I'm half expecting to be called out of the lesson. That the lads will have been caught red-handed and will have dobbed me in. But when the bell finally goes, I rush out of the classroom and on to the safety of the bus before anyone can stop me.

What I don't see is the grumpy maths teacher finding a discarded poster on one of the tables. I don't see him frowning as he reads the nasty words and I don't see him looking at the image and then taking my drawing out of the bin from yesterday and comparing the pictures and then taking them both straight to Mr Sourden.

By the time I get home, Madeleine and John are in the kitchen, waiting for me.

"Why are you home early?" I ask, as John stares at me.

"Why do you think, Fred?"

His voice is loud and cold. I instantly know that they know about the picture, but just in case it's something else, I decide to play innocent.

"Are you sick?" I ask.

"I am humiliated, Fred. That's what I am. Your mother has been on the phone to the head teacher. Bullying a woman with cancer. You are a disgrace and an embarrassment. Get in the car."

Madeleine bursts into tears. I stand there silently, not knowing what I should do. I agree with them.

I am a disgrace and an embarrassment. I should never have joined in with Callum and his mates. I should never have left Rupert. All of a sudden, my choices feel heavy and wrong. This is bad. Really bad.

It's silent in the car and when we walk into Mr Sourden's office, he sees us and says, "This is Mrs Ketsgrove."

I turn to see the bald lady holding on to one of the posters. She looks tired and sad. Nothing like the angry shusher I saw on the first day.

Mr Sourden talks. Madeleine cries and sobs. John apologizes on my behalf over and over and talks about his time at the Gains and what he wants from his son. Mrs Ketsgrove and me say nothing. When finally there is nothing more for John to say and Madeleine's sobs are quieter, Mrs Ketsgrove says quietly, "Could I talk to Fred alone, please?"

I'm instantly terrified.

When everyone else has left the office, she looks at me.

"I've been a teacher for a really long time," she says. "I think I know kids pretty well by now."

I wait, not knowing if she wants me to say something or not.

"Shall I tell you what I know about you, Fred?"

I wait for her to tell me a long list of how I am the worst kid on the planet. How she has never met a more horrible child.

"I know that you didn't write the words on this poster."

My eyes go wide. She's going to want names. She carries on.

"I know that you probably feel bad about the words on this poster. I know that you ended up hanging out with those boys yesterday and didn't really fit in with them."

I wonder when she's going to start saying all the horrible things about me.

"That's what I saw yesterday at basketball. Do you want to know what I saw today, in here?"

"OK," I say.

"I saw a scared boy who feels like he has no voice. No say in his own life. Am I close?"

I feel a tight knot in my throat and I know that it would be impossible to speak, so I give a little nod. There is a pause and she stands up.

"I see you, Fred."

She looks at me. I can't tell exactly what she is thinking. "You made a bad choice, that's all.

But next time you can make a better one, can't you?"

I nod again and the tears fall from my eyes down my cheeks.

"Oh, and if I were you, I would try and speak to your parents. Maybe stop trying to be someone you're not."

I breathe a sigh of relief. Maybe it's all going to be OK. She's not so bad after all. But then she carries on.

"However," she says calmly, "I also know kids like you don't change unless they have to. Unless they see the consequences of what they have done. Those other boys are unlikely to change. You could, though. But not if you keep making weak and cowardly choices. That's what you are, Fred, a coward. If you learn one thing, I hope that it's to stand up for yourself and to stand up for other people who are weaker than you."

I nod and she walks towards the door.

"Now I have to go home to my family and cuddle my scared children and wipe their tears. Only today it will be even worse because when they ask me about my day, I can't tell them, can I? I can't say that someone hurt my feelings. That someone drew a picture that made me cry in the staff toilet. I have to keep that to myself. So, what you have done, Fred, is make my short, sad life just a little bit worse."

I feel sick, like I might actually vomit. I don't know what to say.

"I'm sorry," I whisper.

She shrugs and sighs, as though my apology means nothing. The scale of her sadness is on full show. She opens the door and goes to talk to Mr Sourden, while Madeleine and John can't even look at me.

Mr Sourden and Mrs Ketsgrove finish talking and he puts his hand on her shoulder as she wipes a tear from her eye. She then turns and walks away. He gestures for Madeleine and John to come back into the office.

"I'm afraid," says Mr Sourden seriously, "Mrs Ketsgrove has decided that she can no longer teach at the school. In no small part because of what happened today. My staff are my number one priority and bullying a staff member, particularly one who is vulnerable, cannot be accepted. I feel I have no choice but to expel Fred. I sincerely hope that he finds another school and behaves in a kinder and more appropriate way."

What on earth is happening? This is worse than I ever imagined. I mean, I know it was bad. Really bad. I should never have chosen the boys and I should never have drawn the picture, but this is too much.

"I'm sorry!" I say, louder than I plan to. "I'm sorry!"

"I am sorry too, Fred, but in this case, I have no choice. The Gains School has a zero-tolerance approach to bullying."

John grabs me by the arm and drags me out of the room, apologizing as we go.

After a completely silent drive home, tears falling from my eyes as though they will never end, John sends me to my room.

"Don't expect to come out of there for a long time, Fred. As long as it takes for us to find a school foolish enough to take you on."

I sit at the bedroom door listening to their voices, hearing sobs and raised tones. Words like "embarrassing", "lesson" and "punishment".

When I have sat and cried my tears out, the image of Mrs Ketsgrove wiping a tear away flashes into my head along with a tight feeling of guilt, like a fist in my chest. I picture her at home with her family. I have never felt so sad and sorry in my life. I created all this. It's all my fault. I think about what will happen next. What school will I go to? Maybe they will send me to Browtree. A spark of hope rises inside, instantly replaced by the guilt. Surely nothing good should come from this? I think about Rupert and how I will never see him again. I think back through all my choices and about what I would have done differently. How would it have ended if I had told Callum where to go? If I had stuck up for Rupert. Where would I be now?

As I sit on the floor, alone in my bedroom, I make a promise to myself. Whatever school I go to, wherever I end up next, if I find a friend even half as kind as Rupert I will stick with them. I pick up my sketchbook and draw a picture. A robot on a bike with a ribbon saying sorry flying out behind him. The first thing I will do if I am ever allowed out of here again is take the picture to Rupert and tell him that I'm sorry.

To find out what happens next, turn to **page 307**.

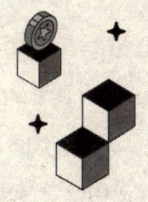

GRAFFITI

Just as I'm about to throw the paint across the room I see Rupert's face through the window in the door. He gives me a thumbs up and a sad smile. Seeing his face takes the heat out of my anger somehow and instead of flinging the paint, I put it back on the table and slump into the chair, burying my head into my arms on the desk.

Rupert comes in and stands next to me.

"She's really trying to sort something out with them, Fred. We've got robotics anyway tomorrow, then I reckon by Friday she will have solved it."

I don't lift my head.

"I hate this horrible school," I say. "I should have got on the other bus."

Rupert sits down next to me.

"What do you mean?"

"I found a jumper for Browtree. That's where I wanted to go. They have the most amazing art department. I was going to get on that bus, but I didn't, because I'm too scared to do anything or say anything that might upset my parents."

"Secretly going to the wrong school sounds a bit extreme, Fred, but you should have told them. You should tell them that you aren't happy."

"You've not met them," I mutter quietly.

"Well, shall I come over after school? See what you're dealing with?"

"Madeleine would have a fit. She thinks she needs to clean for a month before anyone sets foot in the house, even though it's constantly pristine."

"She can't be that bad. I'll just pop in and say hello. Why don't you go and sort yourself out? Wash your face and I'll meet you in the lunch hall. We can have our own art club anyway. You only need paper and a pencil. We can do it in the bogs if we have to!"

I smile and we walk out of the classroom together. As Rupert heads off to lunch, I walk into the toilets. There are a group of boys standing by the sinks. They're massive and one of them has a shaved head. They look dodgy and I immediately feel the threat of their presence. But when I walk in, the biggest one, with a necklace, says, "Let's get out of here, Callum. Are we going to basketball?"

And they shove past me and out of the door.

Inside a cubicle I lock the door and look around the walls of the toilet. Words and tags fill the space.

Gemma loves Leon

YOU STINK

Sam waz ere

PULL MY CHAIN

Baldy Ketsgrove is hot

I see a black Sharpie on the ledge behind the toilet. It feels like a sign. Something telling me that I should add to the graffiti. I should make my voice heard. Maybe Rupert was right. Maybe I can make my own art club anywhere. I feel a rush of excitement at the thought of what I'm about to do.

I click the lid off the pen and without knowing what I'm going to draw I place the tip against the wall of the cubicle. Another rush of adrenaline and excitement. I start drawing a picture of the school from the outside. I get lost in the drawing and time vanishes as my hand moves. The picture grows and grows. The school looks scary and old and has sad faces peering out of every window and kids jumping from the roof. Out in front of the gates stand a row of teachers, all with a speech bubble coming from their mouths.

"NO ART."

"NO JOY."

"NO INDIVIDUALITY."

As I draw it's like nothing else exists. I have no idea how long I have been in here but when I step back and see the drawing, I'm happy. It looks amazing. It fills the entire wall. I smile to myself and click the lid back on to the pen and throw it back on to the shelf.

When I leave the toilet with a spring in my step there is a teacher out in the corridor. He glares suspiciously and I feel a huge crash of dread hit me. What have I done? What if I get caught? Madeleine and John were furious enough about a negative for doodling on some paper. I can't even imagine how bad it would be if they found out about this. I walk as fast as I can towards the hall but when I get there the bell rings and it empties out. I must have been drawing in the toilet for about an hour!

When I sit next to Rupert in history he leans over. "Where did you go?"

"I'll tell you later," I say, still shaking with adrenaline. "I think I might have made a terrible decision."

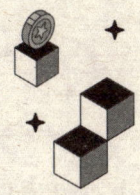

RUPERT COMES HOME

When the bell goes at the end of the day, I take Rupert to show him my graffiti.

"It's an amazing drawing, Fred, but I'm not sure it was a good idea."

"I know. What should I do?"

At that moment we hear the door open and the caretaker's bucket crashes into the toilets.

"Let's get out of here!" Rupert whispers and we scramble out of the cubicle and past the caretaker as quickly as we can. When we are out of view we sprint. Behind us, we hear the caretaker shouting after us, "Oi, you two!"

We run even faster.

"Shall we grab a bike and ride to yours again?"

"Yeah." I nod. The last place I need to be right now

is on a school bus. I need to clear my head. "Can we ride down past the sea?" I ask.

"Sure."

On the bike, as the wind blows into my face, I almost forget about everything. The art room being closed doesn't matter any more and the graffiti has vanished. All that feels important is the salty air and the sea.

As soon as we get to my house, reality sets in. Rupert is about to meet my parents. I never bring friends to my house. I did once in primary and Madeleine was so stressed and weird the whole time, offering us snacks and then hoovering around our feet as we ate them. She will be so cross that I didn't give her any warning, but maybe this is the best way and Rupert is so nice that maybe he will charm her out of being too weird.

"She can be pretty uptight," I say, just before I open the door.

"It's fine, honestly. Everyone's families are strange in some way."

I look at him and shake my head. He has no idea.

When we are in the house and taking our shoes off, I can hear the hoover coming from the front room.

"Put your shoes in this shoe hole. This one is for guests."

"Wow, this is organized! You should see our shoe pile!"

We go into the house and Rupert stares at the beige carpets and tidy surfaces.

"It's like a magazine," he whispers.

"A pretty boring magazine, if you ask me."

I go to the front room and Madeleine is lying on the floor with the hoover pipe under the sofa. When she stands up, we are both smiling at her from the doorway.

"Oh my god!" she shrieks and puts her hand to her heart. "What on earth are you doing, Fred? You nearly gave me a heart attack."

She turns the hoover off and smooths her hair, looking at Rupert and clearly wondering who this is in her house.

"This is my new friend Rupert," I say. I'm panicking now. I hope she's nice to him and I don't get into trouble for bringing him home.

"Hello, Mrs Timple," Rupert says, holding his hand out from his long sleeve. "Have you had a nice day so far?"

Madeleine shakes his hand and gives a tight smile.

"Yes, thank you, Rupert. It's very nice to meet you."

Then she turns to me.

"If you had given me any warning at all, Fred, then I wouldn't have been squished under a sofa when you got home and I would have made enough snacks for both of you."

I can see that she is worrying. Wondering what she will give us to eat and how long he is staying. I let her off the hook.

"We're just going to hang out in my room. We don't need snacks and Rupert will be gone before tea. OK?"

She looks visibly relieved.

"OK, boys. I will carry on with this, then. Call if you need me, but maybe don't sneak up on me next time!"

"She's nice!" Rupert says, as he flops on to my bed.

"Yeah, she is nice. Just on the edge of a nervous breakdown at all times."

"Why don't you call them Mum and Dad?" he asks. "And where is all your stuff?"

"They don't like being called Mum and Dad and this is all my stuff – apart from my artwork. I hide that behind Madeleine's pictures. Look."

I turn the pictures round and reveal all my

drawings. Rupert looks carefully through them.

"These are so good," he whispers, as he brushes his fingers lightly over one of my favourites. "But why are they hidden? You either hide your art here or in the toilets at school!"

"Well, I'm not allowed to do it here and now I can't do it at school either. It's so unfair."

"I've been thinking about the graffiti," Rupert says. "I think you need to own up."

"WHAT?" I say. "No way!"

"Didn't you say there was a teacher outside when you came out of the loo?"

"Yeah, but he wouldn't have known anything."

"What about when he checks the cameras?"

"What cameras?"

"They have cameras in the corridor outside the toilets to check who has gone in and out. It's meant to stop bullying ... and vandalism."

I slump down on the bed next to him.

"Oh no."

"They might not check, but I reckon when the caretaker tells them about the drawing, that's the first thing they'll do. You could just wait and see but if you own up, explain about the art room and say sorry, they might go easier on you."

"Either way, they'll tell my parents, though, won't they?"

Rupert nods.

"If it were me, I would tell Madeleine tonight before she gets a phone call, but it's your choice. You never know, you might get away with it. But don't you think you should talk to your folks anyway? About hiding all your art? They need to know what it means to you."

"They won't listen," I say.

Rupert shrugs and carries on looking through my drawings. When Madeleine knocks on the door, I grab all the drawings and paintings and shove them under the bed. The door opens and her face peers in.

"How is Rupert getting home? I'm worried about him. Do your parents know where you are? I should really have your mum's number."

Rupert gets up.

"Don't worry, Mrs Timple. I texted my mum to let her know I was here. I'm going to head back now; I've got a bike."

As Rupert is getting his shoes on, John comes through the door.

"Whoa, it's like Piccadilly Circus in here. Who are you?"

"I'm Rupert. I'm going home now."

"Well, bye, Rupert!" When he has gone, John turns to me. "You didn't meet him on the basketball team, did you? He's tiny!"

As he laughs to himself, I get a glimpse of the kind of kid my dad might have been. I'm not sure he would've been as kind as Rupert.

"He's in my class," I say. "He's really nice."

"I'm sure he is… Just don't ask him to reach anything from a high cupboard!" Then he heads upstairs to get changed, like he does every day.

When we all sit down to tea, my heart is racing. I'm thinking about what Rupert said. I know that he's right. It's better to come from me rather than just waiting to be caught. I keep trying to say something. Trying to find the words to start the conversation but nothing comes out. I don't even know where to begin.

I listen to them clinking their cutlery and chatting about John's work and where we might go for our next holiday. By the time they are getting to their last mouthful, I've not said a word. How does Rupert make it sound so easy? To just talk. To tell the truth.

"Are you OK, Fred? You look a bit pale," Madeleine says, as she places her knife and fork on her empty plate. This is it. This is my chance to tell them. To make the right choice and try and make this awful situation just a teeny-tiny bit easier. It doesn't feel easy, though. I'm just about to do what I always do. To pretend that I'm fine and clear up the plates. To let things carry on the way they are, the way they have always been. Ignoring the truth and ignoring the important things that need to be said. But something is different tonight. I have got a minute bit of strength and courage from somewhere deep down that allows the words to come out, even though they are in a whisper.

"I made a mistake today," I say. "A pretty big one."

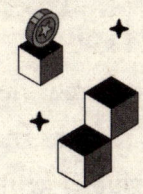

TELLING THE TRUTH

"Pardon, darling? You're mumbling again," Madeleine says, as she stands to clear the table.

"I did something bad. You're going to be really angry," I say, a little bit louder now. Madeleine frowns and sits back down.

"What on earth are you talking about, Fred?"

I sit there, looking at their faces, and I'm not sure how to carry on.

"Spit it out, Fred," John says. "Don't keep us waiting."

I try and think about how it all started. I need to go back to the beginning.

"I didn't join the basketball team," I say. "I didn't want to even go to the Gains School."

"Well, what team did you join?" John says.

"I joined art club," I say.

"For goodness' sake, Fred," John huffs. "You and those silly doodles. I'm sure that you can join art club *and* basketball club, I will have a word with Mr Sourden. Is that it?"

"No, that's not it," I say, feeling a bit stronger now that I've started. "I went to art club and I loved it, but today they stopped it. They closed the art room and it was the only thing that I liked in that school, apart from Rupert. I got really angry and I did something bad."

They both sit in silence, the realization that I might be in trouble slowly sinking in.

"It felt really unfair. It's the thing I love the most and I know you think it's silly, but I want to be an artist. I was angry at the school and at you, and at everyone for not letting me do the thing I love."

"What did you do, Fred?" John's voice is low and slow.

"I drew a picture," I whisper.

"Go on."

"On the toilet wall."

Madeleine gasps and puts her hands over her mouth. John rolls his eyes.

"I'm really sorry, and I know it's bad. I will tell

school and clean it off or whatever, but I can't stop drawing. I have been hiding my art from you for months."

"What do you mean, hiding it?" John says. "You'd better not have drawn on any of our walls!"

I tell them to follow me, and upstairs I turn round every picture on the walls and take all the drawings out from behind the pictures and under the bed. There are hundreds.

Madeleine sobs and John looks through them.

"Why would you hide them?" he says.

"Because you hate that I love art."

They look confused and I know I have to explain. I have to try and make them understand.

"Madeleine throws all my pictures away. I'm not allowed to paint or draw or make a mess. I am not allowed to be myself. I know I'm not what you want. I know you want a kid that's just like you. That plays sport, gets good grades and keeps his room immaculate but I'm not that kid. I'm sorry. I'm just different from you, that's all." I feel sad and guilty for not being the kid they want but a big wave of relief washes over me. Relief at having said it, of showing them the pictures and telling them the truth.

There's a silence as they look at the drawings.

I can feel the hope inside me build as I crave their acceptance, but then John sees one that is clearly of him and Madeleine. Clocks and timers going off all over the drawing and them like zombies going from one task to the next. He turns it over to face the bed and then looks up at me.

"You are no artist, Fred. Your little hobby has got out of control. *You* are out of control and I will see to it that you are in detention for the rest of the year. You will repaint the toilet and apologize to Mr Sourden and there is still a good chance you will be expelled. You have made some terrible choices, Fred, and you will see the consequences."

"I know. That's why I told you, to try and make it better."

"Too little too late, Fred. You can't backtrack. There are no do-overs in real life. Now clean up these doodles and say sorry to Madeleine."

"Sorry, Madeleine," I say, as she sobs and follows John out of the room.

I take out my phone and message Rupert:

> That didn't go well.

> ???

> They hate me even more AND I've got to paint the toilets.

> You would have been in more trouble if they had found out from school. Did you talk about your drawings?

> Yeah. They hated them.

> At least they know about them now. Just keep trying. When the graffiti is gone and everything has settled you can talk to them again. Well done for owning up!

I sigh and flop down on to the bed. Nothing feels sorted. I want things to be different, but I just don't know how. I start piling up all my drawings and wonder why I'm even keeping them. Maybe Madeleine is right to throw them away. What's the point? Then I hear a small knock at the door and Madeleine pokes her head round.

"I'm really sorry, Madeleine," I say.

"I know you are. John will take a while, but he'll be OK. He's talking to Mr Sourden and I don't think you will be expelled."

Then she holds something up.

"I found these and thought they might be useful?"

She opens up a bag with some empty white picture frames in it.

"I never used them and I thought maybe you might like them."

"What for?" I ask.

"Your pictures, of course. We don't want them looking scrappy, do we?"

I look at her and she looks nervous, as though this is all new and she's not sure how to act. I smile, as I realize that this is all new to me too. New but nice.

"No. We definitely don't want them looking scrappy," I say.

"I thought you liked the boats, but you can swap them if you like."

As she leaves the room, I feel a tiny bit of hope light up inside me. Maybe telling them and showing them who I am was the right choice. Maybe if I just keep trying, like Rupert says, I might find my way. I hold up a frame, allowing a little smile to escape, and I decide which of my drawings I want to put on the wall.

> To find out what happens next, turn to **page 319**.

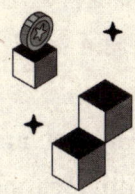

TRASHING THE ROOM

The tears stream down my face and as I imagine all my hidden art at home, I feel another wave of anger take me over. Why should I have to hide my art? If I can't do it at home then I need to do it here. I hate them for taking this away from me. Before I even know that I've made a choice, I see the pot of paint fly across the room. When it hits the wall and a flash of bright red sails through the air and streaks the wall and floor, it feels like some of the rage has been released. I pick up another and launch it into the air. Soon I'm in a frenzy and am flinging anything I can get my hands on. It feels so good, like finally I'm letting it all out.

When I run out of paint, I throw everything on to the floor. I sweep paper and pens and statues into piles by the desks. I turn tables upside down and kick chairs off their legs. I feel free and wild and out of control.

I don't hear the door open and I don't see Rupert and the teachers silently scanning the destruction I have caused. Just as I'm about to turn another desk upside down I hear Rupert's voice, tiny and scared.

"Fred?" he says.

As soon as I hear his voice the feelings subside. The anger leaves me and I come out of my trance and back to reality. I turn and look around the room as though someone else was responsible. Madeleine and John! What will they do when they hear about this?

I look at the teachers and Rupert. I feel hot, wet tears on my cheeks.

"I'm sorry," I sob. "Please don't tell my parents. I'm sorry."

They look scared and sad, as if they are not sure what to say to me or what to do next. Like I'm some kind of animal that might attack if they make the wrong move. I can't cope with the pained look on their faces and so I pick up the tables and start putting everything back.

"Look, I will fix it. I'm sorry. I'm so sorry. I just felt really cross about art club. I don't know what happened. I'm sorry."

As I say sorry over and over again, Rupert helps me pick things up. Then slowly the teachers come and help too. As I watch the room get put back together, I sit on the floor with my head on my knees and cry like a baby. I didn't know that I felt so angry. I didn't know that hiding such a big part of myself would come out in this way. I don't know how to fix this. I don't know how to make it go away.

As though he can hear my thoughts, Rupert comes and sits next to me.

"You'll be OK," he says.

"What about my parents?" I whisper.

"You will be OK," he says again.

But I'm not so sure.

Miss Nolan comes and squats in front of us.

"Now, between you and me, Fred, that's exactly how I felt when they came in here and told me there was no art club."

She smiles and a tiny part of me thinks that maybe I could get away with it. Then she carries on.

"But sadly we can't chuck stuff about when we feel like the world is unfair. Shall I come with you to Mr Sourden's office and we can all have a chat?"

I nod and she helps me up from the floor. Rupert waves at me as we head down the corridor, as though he may never see me again, which I guess could be true.

"Do you want to go and wash your face and get a tissue?" she asks, as we pass the toilets.

"Yes, please."

After I have washed away all the tears I grab some loo roll from a cubicle and see a Sharpie lying on the back of the ledge behind the toilet. I remember when Madeleine and John made me get rid of all my markers. I grab the pen and quickly put it in the front pocket of my bag. I'm not sure what I plan to do with it and why I take it, but it feels good knowing that whatever happens next, it's there. Even if I get kicked out and can never draw again, I have a secret way to make my mark on the world. I head back out to Miss Nolan and we walk down the corridor to see what will happen to me next.

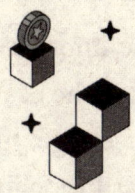

MR SOURDEN

"Wait here," Miss Nolan says, when we get to the head teacher's office. Then she goes inside and I can hear hushed voices coming from behind the door.

"ENTER," calls Mr Sourden's voice and Miss Nolan opens the door and beckons me inside.

Mr Sourden is standing in the middle of the room and looks so tall and still, like a statue or a lamp. When he eventually turns to me, I jump out of my skin.

"Normally, young man, you would be out on your ear. Vandalizing school property during your first week as a Gains student is completely unacceptable."

He looks so stern, I lower my eyes to the floor and wait.

"However, Miss Nolan here seems to be an ally

of yours. Seems to be impressed with your artistic talents. So much so that she has asked for leniency."

I swallow loudly, feeling a huge rush of relief. It might not be as bad as I thought. Maybe they won't tell Madeleine and John; maybe this will all vanish.

"She has suggested that, rather than immediate exclusion, you may need a therapeutic intervention. What do you say to that?"

I'm not exactly sure what he is talking about but it sounds better than being expelled on the spot.

"OK," I say.

"Right, Miss Nolan, you can take him to the counsellor's office and make contact with his parents. They need to come and discuss this issue. When the matter has been discussed, I will speak to the parents about the consequences."

My heart sinks. They are going to find out everything. That I never joined basketball club, that I lied AND that I trashed the art room. Even if I'm not expelled, they will make my life a misery. I feel a new surge of panic and fear and the tears begin again.

"Don't worry," Miss Nolan says. "Let's get you somewhere you can chill out for a bit."

Sitting in an armchair outside pastoral, Miss Nolan goes to make the phone call. I can hear her through the gap in the door and can imagine what Madeleine is saying on the other end of the phone. My heart is beating out of my chest so hard that it almost drowns the sound of her voice but I can just make out the words.

"There has been something of an incident," I hear her say. I imagine the responding gasp from Madeleine. "Fred got a little upset in the art room and made a bit of a mess."

Even though I feel terrible, this makes me smile. It sounds like I might have pooed my pants in an art room. Then as soon as I notice that I'm smiling I shake it off and go back to worrying. This is no time to smile.

"He had every right to feel upset, but we think that maybe he needs to talk to someone about it and we wondered if there may be some other things going on for him. He is at pastoral and will see the counsellor, but we thought that you should come in and talk it through as well? Obviously Mr Sourden has been informed and will want to talk about next steps."

I sigh, knowing that Madeleine will be flapping and breathing hard and unable to cope with any of this information. The silence tells me that she is talking non-stop, Miss Nolan listening patiently.

When she finally finishes, Miss Nolan says, "Well, we will see you and your husband shortly. Don't worry, Mrs Timple, I am sure everything will be fine."

When she comes out, she smiles as if she feels even more sorry for me now that she knows what I'm going to have to deal with.

"Right, Fred, I have a lesson to teach and then will come back in time for when your parents get here. You can go in and have a chat to Heather, the school counsellor. I have filled her in on what happened from my point of view, and she will chat to you a little more before your parents arrive."

As I step into the room, it instantly feels different to the rest of the school. There are two sofas and pictures all over the walls. It feels like a home, rather than part of this terrifying building. I look around the walls at the artwork.

"Do you like my pictures?" says a lady with frizzy greying hair. She's sitting in an armchair by a bookshelf. I give a little nod.

"I wanted to make my little space feel like somewhere people would want to spend time, not just another place to be punished, shouted at or told how to live your life. Sometimes school can feel a bit like you are constantly being told what to do, can't it?"

I nod again.

"Sit down, Fred. How are you feeling?"

I sit on the smaller sofa and look at the floor. It feels really strange in here. So calm. Like it's too nice. She is being too kind. It's so still that I'm waiting for it all to explode. I jiggle my knees and pick my fingernails, not knowing what to say. The silence feels like it goes on for ever. Then the lady speaks again.

"So, my name is Heather and I'm not here to tell you off or get you into trouble. I'm just here to listen and chat. That's my job."

She pauses again and holds out a biscuit tin.

"Do you fancy a custard cream?"

I shake my head. I feel too sick to eat anything.

"Do you want to tell me what happened in the art room?"

I look at her, knowing that I have to speak.

"I don't know," I whisper. "I just felt really angry. I'm sorry."

"No need to apologize to me, Fred. What were you feeling angry about?"

"Not being able to paint. It didn't feel fair."

She listens differently, as though I'm saying a lot more than I really am, and then she nods.

"There are lots of things that feel unfair, aren't there? Why do you think this one made you so cross?"

"Because I want to be an artist and no one will let me."

"No one?" she says, waiting for me to explain. The quiet room and the silence after her question make me want to say the thoughts that come into my brain. To tell her all the things that I haven't told anyone. Whether my parents find out or not doesn't matter in this moment. All that matters is that I tell someone the truth.

"My parents want me to be a different kid to the one I am. I have to hide my art. I didn't even want to come to this school."

She pauses, taking in what I have said.

"OK, so it was about a lot more than the art club. What kind of kid do you think your parents want you to be?"

"Like them."

"And what are they like?"

"Well, they are coming in, so you are about to find out," I say.

She smiles and nods.

"I would love to hear what you think they're like before I meet them, so I can get a good picture. If you could draw a picture of your family right now, what would it look like?"

As soon as she says this, an image starts building in my head and I describe it to her, getting more and more carried away with the detail. When I have described the cleaning products and the clocks and meals on the calendar and the hidden pictures in the bedroom, I feel like Heather has a pretty good idea of what my house is like.

"Well, I think it will be really great for you to talk to your mum and dad about some of these things."

"Madeleine and John," I say.

"Excuse me?"

"They prefer me to call them Madeleine and John."

She pauses, unable to hide her surprise.

"OK," she says. "Well, it sounds like there is plenty to talk about with Madeleine and John."

I smile at her and feel a little bit better knowing that she will be here when they arrive. So much better, my tummy rumbles with hunger.

"Could I have a custard cream actually?" I ask.

"Of course!" she says, holding out the tin. "Take as many as you like."

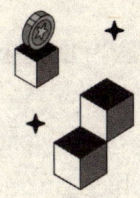

MUM AND DAD

I'm on my third custard cream when they arrive. I can hear them from miles down the corridor. The booming voice of John and the occasional twittering from Madeleine. I shove the custard cream in before they see me. I'm pretty sure they wouldn't think eating biscuits was an appropriate punishment.

I'm completely shocked when Madeleine rushes in and immediately hugs me. She squeezes me so tightly that I can barely breathe. I can't remember the last time we hugged like this.

"Your mother is worried sick, Fred. What on earth has gone on? They said you had some kind of a breakdown."

John doesn't give me a hug and looks cross and suspicious.

Heather stands up and gestures to the sofa.

"Take a seat, Mr and Mrs Timple. Fred's been telling me about some of his worries, and I think that today maybe they bubbled up and got a bit too much to handle."

"What do you mean, worries?" Madeleine asks, grabbing my hand as she sits next to me.

"I'm sorry," John says. "But who are you? Where is Mr Sourden? I would feel much more comfortable discussing this with the head teacher."

"That's fine. We can have a quick chat first and fill you in on what's going on for Fred and you can speak to Mr Sourden afterwards. Would either of you like a biscuit?"

As she holds out the biscuit tin, I try not to smile. She's very good, but I know that she won't be able to calm Madeleine down or stop John from being cross when he hears what I did. Unsurprisingly they don't take a biscuit and after Heather explains what happened, the room is quiet.

"You threw tables and chairs and paint around, Fred?" Madeleine whispers into the silence.

"He was feeling frustrated. I think that art might be more important than you may imagine."

John snorts when she says this.

"Nonsense. You can't chuck stuff about because you're not allowed to scribble on a sheet of paper."

"I think it may be more than scribbling for Fred. The art teacher says that what he painted yesterday was incredibly skilful."

"But it's just art," Madeleine says. "Why did you get so angry, Fred?"

"It's not just art. I was angry at being here. I wanted to go to Browtree. Did you see the art room there? I was angry at the fact I can't draw at home and you make a face or noise if you ever catch me drawing. You call it doodling or scribbling, but I love it."

John frowns so I carry on quickly before he can stop me. I look at Madeleine, who is staring at me and really looks like she is listening.

"I was angry because you don't know any of this and that I can't tell you. I was angry because you tell me who to be, what clubs to join, what to call you, what to eat and I have no say in anything. So when they took this away too, I got really cross."

"Well, this all sounds a bit far-fetched," John says. "You can't sit here and blame us for everything."

"I don't think there's any blame," Heather says. "He's explaining how he feels."

"All this touchy-feely nonsense. In my day you

would be expelled for what you've done, not sat down and given biscuits."

Heather gives me a sad smile.

"All we need to decide," says John, "is what the consequences are and then we will make sure that nothing like this happens again. Mr Sourden is the man for that, and so I thank you for your time, but I think we should go to the head teacher's office now, don't you, Madeleine?"

Madeleine nods and stands up, but as we turn to leave the room, Miss Nolan steps into the doorway.

"Hello, I'm the art teacher, we spoke on the phone."

She holds her hand out to Madeleine. John walks straight past her, but Madeleine stops and whispers, "Do you really think he is talented?" As if it's the first time she has ever even considered it.

"Yes," says Miss Nolan. "Yes, I do."

Madeleine gives a slight nod and then scurries after John. I look at Miss Nolan and then follow them.

When we get to Mr Sourden's office, John goes straight in and tells me to wait outside. Before Madeleine follows him, she turns to me with tears in her eyes.

"Do you really want to be an artist?"

I nod.

"I'm sorry for calling it doodling, Fred."

She holds my hand and then as she goes into the head teacher's office, she whispers, "I will try and fix it, OK?"

I have no idea what she means, but whatever goes on inside the office she must have done something to wind up John and Mr Sourden, as I hear their voices rising. I press my ear to the door and hear snippets of phrases:

"Out of control."

"Lack of facilities."

"Art is not a priority."

"Not like in my day."

"How dare you!"

The volume gets louder and louder until Mr Sourden and John are shouting at each other and I don't need to hold my ear to the door to hear it. Somehow Madeleine has started a war between them and Mr Sourden now thinks I'm a devil child and John thinks the Gains School is a "disgrace".

When they come out, John looks as furious as he sounded. His face is red and he is sweating.

"Stand up, Fred, we are leaving. You are better than this school anyway."

As he storms out of the building I whisper, "What's

happening, Madeleine? Have I been expelled?"

"Not exactly, Fred." Then she whispers, "You wanted to go to Browtree, right?"

I nod.

"Well, I think you might end up at Browtree after all. Don't let me down, Fred. No more outbursts and no more lying."

I nod and she grabs my hand as we follow John to the car.

When we get home, after a completely silent car ride, John says he needs to make some calls and I go and get changed out of my Gains uniform.

"Can I go and get some fresh air?" I ask, knowing exactly where I need to go.

"OK, but not long and be back in time for tea, we are eating at—"

"Six," I say. "I know!"

"There are some things I can change, Fred, but other things will have to stay the same and teatime is definitely one of them."

I smile and head towards the door, then as I look back at Madeleine getting things out of the fridge I run back and give her a huge hug.

"Thanks," I say.

On the way to the beach, I look at my watch. School will just be finished. I text Rupert:

> I'm leaving the Gains.

> So you are on your own in robotics club but can we still go for bike rides?

I see straight away that he's typing:

> How about tomorrow after school?

I send a thumbs up, smile and put my phone in my pocket and run the rest of the way to the beach, knowing the exact spot where I want to be. The place where I can breathe in the air and listen to the waves and nothing else matters.

To find out what happens next, turn to **page 315**.

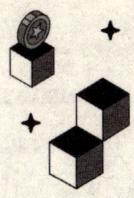

RUNNING AWAY

I call to Marco, "Get up, Marco, we need to get out of here! What are you doing?"

He doesn't look up and the teachers are nearly here. They'll help him, won't they? They will get him out. I take one last look and then I run, down the corridor and out into the yard. My heart is racing. Fear filling my body.

The whole playground is swarming with kids. They look thrilled by the drama of it. I can hear snippets of conversation in the air.

"I heard someone set a jumper on fire."

"Well, I heard a Year Ten smashed a fire alarm."

"I heard Kenny Filkins set a *teacher* on fire."

I walk over to the back of the Year Seven lines and try and stay unnoticed. I hope no one mentions me when they tell the story of what happened. I look towards the school anxiously, hoping to see Marco walk out with a smile on his face.

Five minutes later, when there is still no sign of him and an ambulance pulls into the bus bay, lights flashing, my heart sinks. I should have done something. I should have dragged him out. At the very least I should have stayed with him. Maybe he's still in there; maybe it's not too late for me to help. I take a step towards the school. Should I go back to tell them what happened? Should I have stayed and helped Marco? I'm panicking, my breathing is getting fast and my face is hot. I can't think. This all feels so wrong but should I have stayed and risked getting caught? If I could go back in time, would I still make the same decision or would I change my mind? What would you do?

If you want to **change your decision, go back in time and stay with Marco**, turn to **page 249**.

If you want to **keep going down this path**, then **keep reading**.

The dark excitement of the crowd in the playground builds when the ambulance people get out. A cheer goes up as if it's all a game. As if this is not real and there is not a real kid with a name and a life who I just abandoned in there. More rumours and chatter fly about.

"Someone collapsed."

"A kid couldn't breathe."

"A teacher died."

I almost run after the ambulance crew and follow them into the building, but I stop myself. There is still a chance that everything will be fine. Marco will be fine. I won't be mentioned and no one will find out that I'm at the wrong school.

Finally Marco appears at the doorway with a woman in uniform and the crowd cheer loudly some more. He looks OK but she takes him to the ambulance and they climb into the back. Then Mrs Rumbelow appears in front of us.

"Your teachers will be here shortly to take the register. Once that has been done, we will get you back inside as soon as possible. Everything is under control and there is nothing to worry about, but could everyone in Ash Class please stay outside? We will show you which classroom to go to and we will need to speak to you all individually."

The chatter explodes, everyone figuring out what's going on. As Mrs Machen walks down the line ticking off our names, I know that I need to get out of here. I can't be questioned. No way.

I slip into the line next to us and then move further away into the one next to that. When I am close to the ambulance, I run and hide behind it. The doors are open and I can hear Marco talking to the lady.

"My asthma was really bad anyway this morning," he says, "so I think I panicked. Everyone just left me."

"Is there anyone at home we can call? We need to get you properly checked out at the hospital. You were in there for just a little while too long."

I feel sick. It's almost like she is talking directly to me. As though she knows I'm listening and she wants to tell me that it's all my fault. That I am a bad person who makes bad decisions.

Marco has a horrible-sounding coughing fit and then whispers, "You can call my sister."

I need to make a run for it. I skulk away from the ambulance and head to the main road. I take a quick look back towards school and see the lines of kids slowly going back into the building. I cross the road and walk away, not knowing where I'm going, what

I will do next, or what to do about the sick feeling of shame growing inside me.

"PSSST."

A sound from the alleyway next to the Chinese takeaway.

"Oi, Frederick."

I turn and see Jared hiding in the alley. I instantly feel the shame transform into anger and hatred for him. Before I even know what's happening, I launch myself at him and take him to the ground. We wrestle awkwardly but he's too strong for me and after a couple of elbows to the face he pins me to the ground.

"What the hell are you doing, Frederick? I thought we had each other's backs."

He is out of breath but still smiling. I think he enjoys all this. The drama of it. I can barely speak as he has his weight on top of me.

"He could be hurt! He's in an ambulance," I finally manage to say.

He gets off me and I sit up and add feebly, "And now I'm definitely caught."

"Caught doing what, Fred? That's what I want to know. Tell me or I might have to pin you to the ground again."

When I tell him everything, he laughs and hoots and shakes his head.

"That's completely awesome, Fred. The things we do for art, eh?"

Then he sits for a moment and says, "Sadly, mate, I think your time is up. I can't see a way out of this, as much as I would love to help you. I think your best option now is to lie low. Run away. Find a den. Do you want to find an empty house?"

"No," I say, shaking my head.

"Up to you, but that's what I'm going to do. Either way, neither of us is going back to that school, that's for sure. It's just a matter of time. I wonder who'll get caught first, Frederick. We're like criminals on the run. My money's on you, I bet you don't even last the afternoon. Good luck, Fred."

We stand up and Jared heads down the road. He doesn't even seem worried. I half wonder about following him but I need to be alone. I need to get Marco's face out of my head. I need to think.

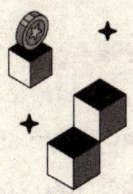

THE LONG WALK HOME

I set off in the opposite direction to Jared and walk down a road that I think takes me towards the beach. I don't want to look at my phone. The idea that it might ring at any moment makes me feel sick, so I switch it off and just walk.

I think about what has happened and what could be happening now. They will have taken the register and seen that me and Jared aren't there. The other kids will be telling them what happened. Will they say it was me and Jared? Surely they will be telling them that I tried to stop him. That it wasn't me. Maybe I shouldn't have run away after all. But they would have got me anyway. They would be asking me right now about my parents and where I live.

They would need phone numbers and addresses and I'm not sure I have many more lies in me.

As I walk aimlessly down street after street, the image of Marco flashes into my thoughts. My legs eventually feel tired and I realize that I might be heading in completely the wrong direction. I could be miles from home or from the beach or from anywhere I recognize. I perch on a wall outside a house with a front garden full of bicycles. It looks like there are nearly fifty bikes and bits of bikes. I wonder what kind of person lives inside. Then when I can't think of anything that will help, I take out my sketchbook and draw a house made of bicycles.

Drawing makes me feel a little bit better and time vanishes like it does when I get lost in a draw dream. I finish the bike house with people made up of bike parts staring out of the circular window wheels and smile. It's pretty good. Without knowing why, I post it through the letter box of the bicycle house. Maybe whoever lives there might like it. When a drop of rain lands on my nose I zip my coat up and keep walking, trawling through my options of what on earth to do next.

I can't go back to Browtree.

There is no way I can go home and tell my parents the truth.

Then a new thought hits me. If I go home at the same time that school finishes then maybe I could just pretend nothing has happened and keep up the lie that I have been at the Gains all day. Browtree will never be able to find me, will they? Maybe I could just go to the Gains tomorrow. Get on the bus I was supposed to get on in the first place. Tell them that my dad changed his mind. I could send another email tonight! Maybe this is the answer.

I feel a jolt of sadness as I realize that I will never get to use the art room of Browtree again but maybe this way I won't get into any trouble and I will be doing exactly what my parents wanted in the first place. I have to get home and send the email and get ready for my first day in that terrifying school as a Gains boy!

I switch on my phone and pull up the map. I'm about an hour away from home. It's only midday, though, so I have another three and a half hours to kill until I can put my blazer on, go back and carry on the lies. I half think about going back and taking one of the bikes from the front garden. I could ride down the beach on that rather than walking around all afternoon but I don't need to add thieving to my list of bad choices.

I feel my tummy rumble. I'm so hungry and the rain is now really coming down. I remember that I have some snacks in my bag. I just need somewhere dry to eat them and hang out until it's time to go home. I can't sit in the rain all afternoon.

I pick up my pace and know where I'm going to go.

When I finally get to the seafront and walk down past all the houses, I see the *For Sale* sign in the distance. Sneaking round the back on my own feels even more dangerous than it did when I was with Jared. I peek into the windows and it's empty and dark. When I get to the shed the door is still wedged open and so I duck in out of the rain and sit on an old car tyre.

My stolen lunch is quite random. There were only certain things I thought I could get away with. Things that Madeleine wouldn't have counted. I take them all out of my bag and spread them on my knee.

A satsuma, a handful of raisins, a slice of bread and two Weetabix. It's not exactly a meal, but I'm so hungry after all the walking, I start shoving things into my mouth. Eating Weetabix with no milk is incredibly dry, so I combine the satsuma pieces and mouthfuls of Weetabix and it ends up tasting pretty good. When I've finished, I dust the crumbs off my trousers and remember that I need to get back into my uniform before I head home.

The shed's pretty small and as I have nothing else to do I figure I might as well tidy it up a bit and make myself a bit comfier. I wheel out the old lawnmower and put it in the garden. Then I pile up the tins of paint by the door. There's a little tool bench hidden underneath cardboard boxes and broken old tools and when I clear it off it looks like a desk. I shove all the dusty, broken things into a box and put it outside. I start getting really into it. It feels like I'm making a little home. I get why Jared likes finding dens now. Although I wonder if he has ever tidied up any of his abandoned buildings.

When the space is finally clear, I look around. I've put an old crate by the desk and it is the perfect height for a chair. There was a dusty old rug all rolled up and covered in cobwebs which is now out on the floor. I look at the walls and wish I had all my hidden art to stick up. It feels like it could be my little art studio. Then I see the paint pots and smile to myself. I have two hours, four empty walls and lots of paint.

A couple of hours later, I'm grinning from ear to ear. I am surrounded by a mural that covers every inch of wall and even goes up on to the ceiling. There are huge waves and houses made of bikes and schools that are on fire. There are buses splitting in two and roads leading to a million different places.

I'm completely covered in paint, but I don't care one bit. That was one of the best things I have ever done, and even if I made the wrong choice in getting on that bus and sitting with Jared, maybe it was all worth it for this moment.

When I get changed and head home, trying desperately to get the paint off my fingers on the way, the feeling that it was all worth it vanishes the moment I get to the house. Two male police officers are standing at the door and Madeleine is crying.

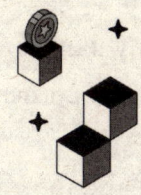

THE POLICE

I quickly duck behind a wheelie bin and peek out from the side. What's going on?! The sick feeling is fully back and has taken over my whole body. I feel so guilty for everything. For leaving Marco and then for forgetting about it enough to paint a shed. What kind of person am I? Why are the police on my doorstep? Did someone watch me painting the shed? Did Marco die and the police are hunting down the suspects? Why is Madeleine crying?

I stay behind the bin, desperately trying to think of what to do and how to handle this. I half wish that Jared was here; he would definitely know what to do. I watch as the police officers go inside the house and I turn and sit on the wet pavement, leaning against the bin. I can feel the water soaking through my

Gains trousers into my pants and so I stand up. As I do, John's car turns the corner and screeches to a stop as he sees me.

He doesn't even park the car but stops in the middle of the road, opens the door and shouts, "Where the hell have you been?"

He is louder than I have ever heard before and there are veins coming out of his neck. "Me and your mother have been worried sick."

I look around as if somewhere in the air an adequate answer will just appear and drop into my brain. But before I can say anything, John grabs my shoulder and pushes me towards the house.

"He's here, Madeleine," he calls, and Madeleine and her sobs come running at me and grab me into a squeeze.

"Fred, I was so scared, where have you been?"

The two police officers are now standing at the bottom of the stairs and looking at me.

"You've had everyone worried sick, Fred," one of them says. "Come on in and tell us what's been going on."

I take my shoes off extra slowly, aware that they are all still watching me. I need some time to figure out what's going on before I say anything. I try to delay by rearranging the shoe holes but John is having none of it.

"Get up, Fred! For goodness' sake. Get in there."

He points to the kitchen and we all go and sit at the table.

"So, where have you been, Fred?" the smaller police officer says calmly.

"School?" I say, testing out what their response will be.

"Which school?" says the police officer.

I look down at my blazer. I don't know what else to say. I don't know how to stop lying.

"The Gains?" I whisper.

"Then what's this?" John roars, as he throws down a printout of the email that I sent to the head teacher at the Gains School.

"Listen, Fred," says the small police officer. "As you don't seem to want to tell us what's been going on, shall we tell you what we know and then you can fill in the gaps?"

I nod and then listen to them explain that my email had raised alarm bells as it did not seem like "the kind of email sent by a parent". I feel instantly annoyed as I thought it was perfect and sounded exactly like John. Then they tell me that Mr Sourden had rung my parents and told them I was not there. Then the big policeman carries on the story.

"We were also contacted by Browtree High about a missing student who they had no valid contact information for. A Fred Timple. So, we know that you were at Browtree. We know that there was a fire and that you ran away. One student was left behind."

Madeleine wails when she hears this. I look at John who looks disgusted. How will they ever forgive me for any of this?

"What we don't know is why you were there in the first place and where you've been all day since you ran away. If you tell us the truth now, Fred, it will all be so much easier. You are not actually in any trouble with us, we just needed to find you."

"Is Marco OK?" I ask.

"Is that the boy you left to burn?" John shouts. "He's OK, but no thanks to you, Fred. What kind of boy are you?"

There is a heavy silence as I bite the inside of my cheek so hard I can taste the blood inside my mouth. I want to shrivel up and vanish.

"What were you doing at Browtree in the first place?" Madeleine sobs.

"I just really wanted to go there instead," I say

quietly. "So I got on the bus. I ran away this morning because I knew they would figure it all out, that I wasn't meant to be there. If Jared hadn't started the fire, it would have all been OK."

"It would most definitely not have been OK," yells John. "I don't think you understand, Fred, how worried we've been. How dangerous your actions were. You can't just go to any old school you like and lie to us. Starting fires and running away. This just isn't you."

"I didn't start a fire," I say.

The small police officer can see that John is getting more and more cross and so he carries on in his calm, quiet voice.

"So, where have you been today, Fred?"

"Just walking," I say, and then I picture the shed and another wave of guilt swamps me. I know that I have to tell them. That if I don't, they will find out and it will just get a whole load worse.

"When it started raining, I hid out in a shed."

"What shed?" John hisses.

"Where was the shed, Fred?" the big police officer says. "Was there anyone else in the shed?"

I shake my head and then whisper, "I may have painted it a bit."

"Pardon me?" the big police officer says.

None of them can understand what on earth I'm talking about and so when the policemen ask me to take them to the shed, I'm almost relieved. Even though I might get arrested for vandalism or breaking and entering or whatever, a teeny-tiny part of me can't wait to show them. I can't wait to see the walls again.

When we get there and I show them inside, I hear Madeleine breathe in sharply and John stares around in complete confusion.

The small police officer says, "You did all this today?"

"Yeah, this afternoon." Then I add, "Will I go to jail?"

"Well, I don't think you will go to jail, kid … art school, maybe, but not jail. We will have to contact the owners and see what they want to do about it. They may want to press charges. Did you break into the shed?"

"No, it was open," I say.

"Was it your paint?"

I shake my head. "No, it was already there."

"Well, let's see what they say. Hopefully they're art lovers."

I have to answer quite a lot more questions and they write everything down on a little pad. When the police eventually get up to leave, I'm exhausted. John and Madeleine have been weirdly silent since they walked into the shed.

"We will give you a call in the next couple of days to let you know what will happen next."

Then the small police officer turns as he is walking out of the door.

"You have real talent there, son. But maybe next time paint on your own walls rather than someone else's, eh?"

When the door is closed, John huffs. "Talented, my backside. You are a criminal. I don't know what's happened to the police force. And I don't know what has happened to *you*, Fred. If they aren't going to come up with a suitable punishment for all this nonsense, then I will. Get to your room and do not come out until I say so."

An hour later Madeleine brings me some dinner on a tray. She has stopped sobbing and seems calmer than usual. Maybe there is only so long that you can cry.

"He's really cross, Fred."

"I know. I'm sorry."

"Why did you do it?"

I sit with the tray on my knees and think about the question. I just want to tell the truth after so many lies.

"Because I want to be an artist and I knew you wouldn't let me. Browtree had the best art room ever and I found a jumper and the bus came and I just got on it. I'm really sorry."

"Well, John has been on the phone to the Gains. They have said they won't accept you now, after all this. They called you a criminal."

"Where will I go?"

"Who knows, Fred. Not back to Browtree, that's for sure. If your father has anything to do with it, you would be going to some kind of boot camp for naughty boys."

My shoulders slump and I feel completely pathetic. What horrible place will I end up at now?

As if Madeleine can read my thoughts, she says, "This has all happened because of the decisions you made."

"I know. I'm sorry."

When she stands up to leave, she says, "Oh, yes, and whatever that policeman said, if you ever paint on my walls I will kill you, you know that, don't you?"

I nod and when I look up I think I see the hint of a smile. She pauses on her way out and looks at me.

"Your painting was beautiful, Fred. It really was."

I look up and smile.

"What I can't understand, though, in all this, is how you could have left that poor boy. The bus and the school were silly and thoughtless, but leaving that boy. It's unforgiveable, Fred."

I understand, here in this moment, that however much I want something or however talented or artistic I am, none of it means anything if I'm not kind. The first time that Madeleine has ever noticed my art, thought it was beautiful, has been ruined. By me. Overshadowed by one cruel and selfish decision.

She closes the door and a tear leaks out of the corner of my eye.

To find out what happens next, turn to **page 335**.

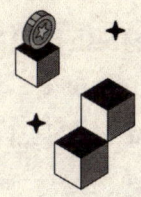

THE RESCUE

I watch Jared disappear and I know that I can't be like him. The teachers are nearly here and they will look after Marco, but that's not the point. A little voice that is so quiet, in another life I may not have even heard it, tells me that I have to stay. I have to do something. I can't leave someone who is struggling. What kind of person would I be if I made a decision to do that?

I run back into the classroom and grab Marco under the armpits. He lets me heave him out of the room and we get to the corridor just as Mrs Rumbelow appears. I keep my arm wrapped around Marco. He feels heavy, like he might collapse. His breath is shallow and fast. I look back into the room and the fire is getting smaller and the smoke is clearing slightly.

"Let's get you some fresh air," Mrs Rumbelow says. "The ambulance is on its way."

Marco shakes his head. "No, I can't go to hospital," he wheezes.

"They will need to check you out. You are not breathing properly. Do you have asthma?"

He nods and Mrs Rumbelow walks into the classroom with her arm over her face and points to Marco's bag, which is still on the floor.

"Is this his?" she asks me. I nod and she brings it out into the corridor. "Do you have an inhaler?"

"Yes," he says and she opens the bag and rummages through until she finds it. She passes it to Marco and then asks us to follow her. We go down to her office and she opens up the back doors so that we can sit outside.

"I think you will be better here than having everyone stare at you in the playground, don't you? The ambulance should be here very soon. I will get us all a little drink and a biscuit, and you just keep breathing and try to stay calm."

I'm amazed at how calm *she's* being. I wonder if you have to take tests at staying calm to be a teacher. I imagine Madeleine in this situation. She would be gasping, panicking and screaming, telling us all to run for our lives. I look at Marco, who is coughing a bit less now.

"Are you OK?"

"Yeah, it's my asthma. It makes me panic when I can't breathe."

"It sounds horrible." Then I pause for a second and add, "Sorry I didn't sit with you yesterday."

"That's OK," he says. "I'm OK on my own. I'm pretty used to it."

Then he has another coughing fit. Mrs Rumbelow comes out with some juice and biscuits.

"OK, boys, the paramedics are just pulling in. They will get you checked out and fixed up in no time. What's your name, sweetie?" she says to Marco.

I know that she will ask me next and I half think about getting up and sprinting away but my legs don't move and when she turns to me and asks, I reply quietly, "Fred Timple."

"Ah, the mysterious Fred Timple! We've been looking for you. We need to get in touch with your parents and here you are, busy rescuing people!"

I smile and then hear a cheer go up from the crowd in the playground and a few seconds after that the ambulance crew appear in their uniforms and smile at Marco.

"So, I'm guessing it's you we are here to see?"

As they ask some questions and listen to his chest, Mrs Rumbelow takes me to one side and says, "Right, Fred, the fire is out now. I'm going to quickly go and tell everyone in the playground what's happening and then I will be back to give your folks a call and let them know what a hero you are."

When she has gone, I look over at Marco and see the ambulance people leading him away.

"Is he OK?" I call after them.

"He'll be fine. We are just going to check him out properly in the ambulance and give his family a call."

I sigh and go and sit on one of the chairs, waiting for the inevitable. For my parents to find out what a liar I am and for my whole life to fall apart.

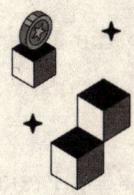

MRS RUMBELOW

When Mrs Rumbelow comes back, I'm pacing around her office like a caged tiger.

"Are you OK, Fred? It must have been quite a shocking morning for you. Marco is fine. His sister is coming. Do you want to tell me what happened this morning and then we can call your parents? If you want to go home for the rest of the day, I completely understand."

I shake my head and she gestures to the chair and I sit down.

"So, we have spoken to some other members of Ash Class and the stories all match up. We've not been able to find Jared, so if there is anything you know about him or where he may be, that would be very useful."

"He likes hanging out in empty houses," I say quietly. "I sat next to him instead of Marco. I should have chosen Marco."

"Well, we all make mistakes," she says. "You certainly made up for it by looking after Marco so well this morning, didn't you? Do you know what empty house he may be in?"

I shake my head again.

"OK, not to worry. The police are out looking for him so that's not our problem any more. Now on to you, Fred, we don't seem to have any information at all for you."

"I wasn't meant to come here..." I say.

"Pardon me?"

"We visited when we moved house, but I was supposed to go to a different school."

She frowns a little and then smiles.

"So you applied late? You just moved here, yes? Maybe Mrs Petts didn't add you to the system, although that would be out of character for her."

She starts looking through files and opening drawers.

"You won't find anything," I say. "I'm not supposed to be here."

She stops looking at her files and turns to look at

me as though she's realized that there is a problem.

"What do you mean, Fred?"

I don't know why, but I tell her everything. I tell her all about the jumper and the bus. I tell her how scary the Gains School was and how much I loved the art room here. I tell her that when the bus arrived it felt like a sign and that I want to be at this school more than anything. She sits and listens with her chin in her hands as if I'm telling her the most interesting story in the world. When I finally get to the end, there is a silence and it feels so good to have told someone. Even though I know Madeleine and John will kill me, it's a relief to get it all out and have someone listen.

"Wow," she says after a while. "I have been teaching for a long time, Fred, and I thought I'd seen it all. Turning up at completely the wrong school, that is something else."

I smile and shrug, not really knowing what else to do.

"Did you ask your parents if you could come here? Why did they send you to the Gains if you wanted to be here?"

"It's not really their vibe," I say. "They like rules and uniform and sports clubs and exams, they're not so much into art and stuff."

"Hmmm. I see," she says, and then she sits quietly and stares into space for a while. She occasionally starts to say something but then she stops herself and carries on staring at nothing. Eventually she runs out of false starts and some words come out.

"I really don't want you to get into too much trouble, Fred, but I can't see a way out unless..." She pauses. "I do have a good friend at the Gains."

She scratches her chin and takes out her phone.

"Let me make a couple of calls. Do you think it would make a difference who spoke to your parents?"

I shrug. "Not really. Madeleine will cry and John will shout and I will be in blazer and tie at the Gains tomorrow probably."

"Are they your parents? Madeleine and John?"

I nod.

"You don't call them Mum and Dad?"

"They don't like it," I say, and I feel like I have flown outside my body and can see myself saying these words in this office, sitting in this chair. I can see how miserable it sounds and how worried Mrs Rumbelow must be for me. I realize that my life is not normal. That it's not normal to call your mum and dad by their names. I want to have a life where I can make decisions and I want a life where I can go to whatever school I want and paint murals in outdoor corridors. Maybe sometimes I would make the wrong choices, but I want to live a life where that doesn't feel so scary. Where it's OK to be me and to listen to the little voice inside me that tells me what is right ... even if I don't always hear it in time.

"Well, give me their number and I will make a couple of calls and we will see what happens, but just so you know, Fred, I would love to have you here at Browtree."

When I have given her the number she taps the digits in and I'm so glad that she is the one doing the talking. When she holds the phone up to her ear she says, "Hello, is that the Gains School? I'd like to speak to Heather, the school counsellor." Then she gives me a wink and leaves the office. I sit and wait, wondering what on earth she is doing.

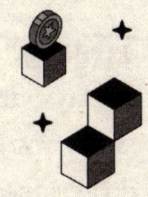

THE GAINS

When she comes back in, she's smiling.

"So, we think we may have a plan, Fred. It still involves telling your parents everything, obviously, but it may be better if that happens at the Gains rather than here, don't you think? Then your parents will be slightly less wrong-footed and we can come up with a solution all together. Heather is wonderful and it will be good for you to meet her anyway. If you end up at the Gains, she will look after you, I promise. Let's go. She is contacting your parents now."

I feel like I might be sick. The idea of going back to that school and Madeleine and John being there too and hearing about all this makes me shudder. Mrs Rumbelow can sense my fear.

"Just so you know, Fred, I get it. We will be with you, but at the end of the day, only you can speak out and tell your parents what you really want. That's what you will have to do at some point."

I nod, knowing that I will not be able to tell my parents anything after they find out about all this. They will be too angry to listen. She gets her coat and takes me out into the car park. As we drive over to the Gains I stare out of the window and try to catch glimpses of the sea.

Madeleine and John have been told the whole story, and by the time they arrive at the Gains, they are furious.

"How on earth could this possibly happen?" screams Madeleine.

"I have every intention of suing the lot of you!" John says. "My son has been at the wrong school for over twenty-four hours and no one seemed to notice anything was wrong. It's outrageous."

I hadn't imagined that they would be more angry at the school than with me. I keep silent and try to make myself smaller so they don't notice me.

The counsellor, Heather, asks them to sit down, and when they refuse and keep shouting, she calls the head teacher.

"We had hoped that we could have a calm conversation about the possible reasons for Fred wanting to attend Browtree, but I see now that won't be possible," she says, holding the phone to her ear.

"Mr Sourden, the Timples are in my office. You can come and see them now." Mrs Rumbelow smiles at me sadly as though she now realizes her plan to try and make it better may not have been her greatest ever idea.

When Mr Sourden glides into the room John immediately calms down a bit, as though he's a child again and this is his head teacher.

"Mr and Mrs Timple, you must be most upset. I can tell you now that we were about to call you when Mrs Rumbelow contacted the school, as we had a suspicious email, which I now believe to have come from your son. It seems that he was going to great lengths to keep his secret. Now that I know what kind of child he is, we will keep a close eye on him and call you immediately if anything suspicious happens in the future. Obviously there will need to be consequences for his actions, which we can discuss."

Mrs Rumbelow looks disappointed, and Heather adds, "I would like to see Fred every day to see how he is settling in. I would also suggest that we introduce him to Miss Nolan, the art teacher, as Mrs Rumbelow has said that art is his passion and was one of the main reasons for his desire to attend Browtree."

She pauses and looks at Madeleine, hoping that she'll see a glimmer of understanding. Madeleine just sobs.

"Fine," John says. "You can talk about your feelings all you want with him in here, but if he ever doesn't turn up at this school again, I expect a phone call immediately, do you understand?"

Mr Sourden nods and John puts his arm around Madeleine.

"Fred, we will see you after school. I can't tell you how disappointed we are in you. I had to leave work early to come to this meeting, which my boss won't be impressed about, let me tell you."

Mrs Rumbelow walks out with them and I hear her say, "Fred was actually a bit of a hero this morning. He risked everything to help out another student in need. I really think he is a wonderful child."

"So wonderful he lied to his parents."

She looks back into the room and gives me a little wave.

"Well, we were happy to have him at Browtree, that's for sure. I think it may be worth talking to him when the dust has settled and see what he has to say."

I spend the rest of the morning in Heather's office. She gives me biscuits and makes it feel as if I'm poorly and need looking after, rather than like I'm in trouble. It soon ends when she gets a message from Mr Sourden telling her I need to spend the afternoon in detention on my own.

"Come back tomorrow at lunchtime and let me know how you are getting on. There has been an issue with the art room, but Miss Nolan is looking for a new space and you will be able to go and be creative soon, I promise."

After an afternoon in isolation, the bell makes me jump out of my skin. I have no idea how to get to the bus, or where it even stops, and so on my way out of the school I'm rushing and bump into a small kid in a huge blazer.

"Sorry!" I say.

"No problem. You in a rush?"

"Yeah, I don't know where my bus goes from," I say.

He walks out with me and points. "They all go from there," he says. Then he adds, "I'm Rupert, by the way."

"Thanks, Rupert. I'm Fred." I run towards my bus and head home.

When I walk through the door it's as though nothing has happened. Madeleine is cleaning, maybe a little more intensively than normal, if that's possible, and John has gone back to work.

"John will be home for tea. He is furious, obviously. Get out of those clothes, please, and bring me that filthy-looking jumper. John has signed you up for football and rugby club as you missed the sign-up sheet. You should be grateful. Now I don't think we need to speak of this again, do you?"

I shake my head and make my way upstairs.

It's over. My decisions brought me right back to the same place. Doing sports I hate at a school I don't want to be at.

I hear a buzz on my phone, and I see Marco's name when I look down. He's sent a message:

> THANKS. YOU DID THE RIGHT THING

I smile, knowing that I did. The feeling gives me a glimmer of hope. Maybe I can keep listening hard for that tiny voice and maybe it will get a bit louder.

To find out what happens next, turn to **page 331**.

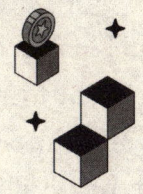

LYING TO MADELEINE

"Don't be daft, Madeleine," I say. "You are such a worrier. A few lads were just talking about some YouTube video about a kid on his own having parties every night. It wasn't about a real kid at school."

I laugh and roll my eyes as if she's dim. She frowns and sighs.

"Well, you know I don't like YouTube. Make sure you don't watch those videos, and probably best to stay away from those boys."

"Yeah, they were idiots. Just older lads. Everyone in my year is really nice," I say.

She smiles. "I'm glad you had a good day. Your father is thrilled about the teams you are on. We are very proud of you, Fred."

I smile and feel sad. I look at Madeleine. *They are not proud of me really*, I think to myself. They're proud of the fake version of me. The one I'm pretending to be. They wouldn't be proud if I showed them the drawing I did at lunch, and they definitely wouldn't be proud if they knew the truth.

"Well, you get on with your homework. Do it at your desk, though, not on your bed. I don't want any pen marks on your sheets."

I nod and she leaves the room.

Maybe it will be fine. Maybe Marco and his sister have it all planned and everything will work out as it's meant to. I can't quite shake the bad feeling inside, though. The full, fuzzy feeling in my head and tummy, like something is not right. The feeling that I may have just made the wrong decision.

The next morning I'm sneaking some snacks into my bag so that I have something to eat at lunchtime. I'm putting a handful of raisins into the zip bit of my bag when Madeleine catches me.

"What on earth are you doing in the cupboards, Fred? Breakfast is all laid out on the table."

"Nothing," I say, my face going red. "I was just looking for ingredients for food tech."

"What ingredients? The school never mentioned this."

She's starting to flap and I need to calm her down.

"It's not for today. I was just checking to see what we had. It's not for a couple of weeks."

"Well, get out of my cupboards, in that case," she says, and swats me away from the kitchen to the table. After I've finished my breakfast, I manage to slip a couple of Weetabix into my bag without her noticing. I'll see what else I can nab on my way out.

When I leave the table, a trail of Weetabix crumbs falls from my lap and Madeleine turns and huffs and gets the hoover out. I run upstairs while she's distracted and pack my spare clothes into my bag and then take the Browtree jumper and creep into Madeleine and John's room.

I hate it in their room. It feels eerily quiet and weirdly empty. I run over to John's dressing-table drawer and get out his body spray. I press the button and cover the mushroomy Browtree jumper and then shove it in my bag.

On my way downstairs Madeleine scrunches up her nose as I walk past and before she can pepper me with any more questions or worries I shout goodbye and am out of the door.

I quickly change my jumper on my way to the bus stop and am wondering how to change into my jeans when I see both buses arrive. I forgot about the bus pass! The driver will not be happy.

As I step on to the bus, I know that another load of lies is about to come out of my mouth.

"Sorry, they ran out of passes at the school office," I say. "They should get some more today, though."

The driver looks at me suspiciously and then nods me on to the bus. I smile and sit in the same spot as yesterday. Lying is getting pretty easy now. You just have to say it with confidence and even if people don't fully believe you, they just seem to go along with it.

I really want to change my trousers but as I'm sitting on the bus trying to cover my legs up and shuffle out of my Gains trousers, kids keep walking up and down the aisle, and every time I panic and have to pull my trousers back up again. This is never going to work. I'll just have to run to the toilets when I get there.

I think that's everything sorted. I go through a checklist in my head. The schools have been contacted. I have kind of got food for lunch and I will get a bus pass today. I can go to art at lunchtime and everything is great. All apart from the nagging feeling I woke with that Marco is in trouble.

When I get to school, Jared, the naughty chair-dancing kid is messing about in form class with some matches. The girls all get really serious and cross with him and luckily when he manages to light some paper near to me and Marco, I'm sitting in the perfect place to put it out quickly before it properly starts. The boy with the matches turns to me and steps towards our desk.

"You are such a try-hard. Don't you want to get out of lessons?"

I try and ignore him, but he's proving pretty hard to ignore. I can sense him standing over me, but before he can do anything one of the girls snatches the matches from his hand and struts away. The boy follows her and starts messing about, throwing bags around the classroom. There are squeals and kids are really getting cross with him but at least it's better than starting a fire.

Marco is coughing and wheezing, even though the paper didn't really light, let alone create any smoke.

"Are you OK?"

"It's my asthma," he says. "It was bad all night."

"Do you have an inhaler or something?"

He nods and takes one out of his bag. "I think it's run out, though," he says, puffing on it. "I've needed a new one for ages."

I know straight away that it must be because his parents haven't sorted him one. He carries on wheezing and when Mrs Machen comes in, she takes the register and stops halfway through.

"Are you OK, young man?"

Marco is really struggling to breathe now and he doesn't answer.

"He has asthma," I say. "I think he needs another inhaler."

She frowns and says, "Take him over to medical, please." Then she looks at him and adds, "Quickly, please."

When we get to medical, the nurse thanks me and sends me back to class. I don't see Marco for the rest of the day. In the art room at lunch, I can't stop thinking about him and I draw a picture of a boy alone in a house.

As soon as school ends, I message him:

> ARE YOU OK? WHAT HAPPENED?

> AM AT HOME.

> ARE YOUR PARENTS THERE?

The three dots that show he is typing pop up and then vanish. I don't hear from him for the rest of the night.

When he's not at school the next day, I know he could be in real trouble.

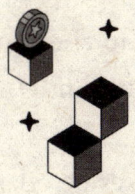

THE MYSTERY OF MARCO

I can't concentrate in lessons and get told off for daydreaming twice. All I can think about is Marco and whether he's OK. If the school don't know that his parents are never around, they won't realize that they sent a boy home to an empty house. That he could have had an asthma attack and be all on his own. How did he even get home? Maybe his parents did pick him up and were with him, looking after him. It's the not knowing that's making me so worried.

By lunchtime I can't cope any more and go to the school office. The lady with the glasses peers over them at me and raises her eyebrows, waiting for me to speak.

"Erm, I just want to check on my friend, Marco Marvel. He's not here and I want to make sure he's OK."

She smiles and takes her glasses off after looking at her computer.

"We have contacted his parents. You are a very good friend to be so worried, I'm sure he's fine."

I try and smile and turn away, but then she asks, "Is there any reason why you are so worried?"

I stop. *Yes*, I think. *There are lots of reasons why I'm worried, but I can't tell you any of them.* I think about my promise to him and his promise to me. I turn back to her.

"He has bad asthma," I say. "Did you actually speak to his parents?" I ask, hoping that she can see the fear in my eyes and that she will do something.

She pauses and for a second I think that she can read my mind but then she puts her glasses back on.

"I've left a message, I'm sure he's fine. You have a lovely day."

Then she goes back to her computer and starts tapping away, the conversation clearly over.

I sigh and make my way to the art room. I try and shove in my two stolen Weetabix as I walk through the outside corridor but they are so dry that I end up spraying crumbs everywhere and a group of sixth-formers stare at me and laugh. Browtree doesn't feel like such a great idea any more. I wonder what I would be doing right now if I had gone to the Gains School. Maybe I would have joined a sports team and become the most popular kid in the year and I wouldn't care that I wasn't allowed to do any art. Maybe I would become the kid that my parents want me to be.

In the art room I paint a picture of a thousand different versions of me. Living all the different lives. Me in a rugby kit and me in front of the iron gates at the Gains. Me being an artist, sitting on the beach, at the dinner table, riding a bike, eating a Weetabix. Then I paint a version of me alone in a house, scared and unable to breathe.

I can't sit here painting when Marco could be in trouble. I have to do something. Even if I can't tell anyone and have to keep my secret. I need to make sure that he's OK. I know exactly where I need to go.

When the bell goes for the end of lunch, instead of walking down the outside corridor and back towards my form room, I walk out and turn left towards the bus bay. I turn to make sure that there are no teachers watching and just see crowds of kids heading into the school. My walk gets faster and faster until I'm running out of school and down the road towards the chip shop.

I bang on the black door until Maisie answers. She looks like she's just woken up and clearly doesn't recognize me at first. She squints her eyes and frowns.

"I'm Fred, remember? Marco's friend. You helped me."

"Oh, yeah. What do you want? It's so early."

"It's half past one," I say. "Anyway, is Marco here?"

"No."

"Have you spoken to him?"

"I picked him up yesterday from school and took him home."

"But are your parents there? His asthma was really bad," I say. "I'm worried about him."

"We are pretty tough, Fred, he'll be fine."

"But I haven't heard from him and he's not at school today. Can we check? Please?"

She seems to wake up a bit when I tell her that he's not at school.

"OK," she says. "Let's go."

On our way to his house she tries calling over and over again and no one answers. She's clearly getting more worried as we get closer and is mumbling things as she listens to the phone ringing out.

"Couldn't they look after him for once?"

"Where do they go? When they leave him?" I ask.

"They go to his dad's."

"His dad?" I ask.

"Yeah, Marco's dad is my stepdad. He has his own flat the other side of town and Mum always goes round there. They're not really bothered about either of us. They think we can look after ourselves after the age of about nine. Not that they were ever much use before then either."

Then she looks at me.

"He shouldn't have told you any of this, though, and neither should I. I'm sorting it. I'm getting him out of there."

"Why don't you live there with him? Then you could look after him."

"There is no way I am going anywhere near them or that house ever again, kid. Now stop asking questions and if anyone ever asks, just tell them everything is fine."

It's clearly not fine, though, is it, and I want to say this. To say that maybe asking for help or telling someone might be the right thing to do. To tell her that shoving everything down and not saying a word will just make everything worse. Then I think about what I've been doing. Maybe I'm not really the one to talk. That's exactly what I've been doing, and look where I am now.

We get to a block of flats and we run up the stairs and she bangs on the door.

"Marco?" she calls, trying the handle and then pushing the door open.

The flat is cold and messy and when we run in, we find Marco sitting on the bed, wheezing. There is no one else here.

"Are you OK?" Maisie asks, putting her arm around him. He shakes his head as he can barely get any breath in. He looks pale and scared.

"I think he needs to go to hospital," I say.

"No," Maisie says. "They will ask too many questions. Anyway, kid, you don't want to be found out for your little school swap, do you, so you'd better go. Leave us to it. We will be fine."

I'm about to turn and go, but then I stop.

"No," I say. "I'm not going anywhere. He's sick and he needs to go to the hospital. Look at him! Marco, tell her."

Marco looks at her and gives a tiny nod of his head.

Maisie lets out a frustrated scream and then calls 999.

"Ambulance, please," she says, holding her head in her hands.

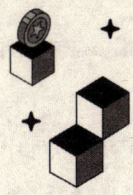

THE HOSPITAL

We sit in silence in the ambulance and when Marco gets wheeled through the hospital, I follow Maisie, even though she turns round and tells me to leave them alone.

"You've done enough!" she snaps.

I'm not sure why she's so angry with me. I'm the one who was looking out for Marco. I don't know what else to do and I want to make sure he's OK, so I follow them into a cubicle and watch as the doctor and nurses put an oxygen mask on to him and do tests and write things down.

"Are you family?" a doctor with kind eyes that look bigger because of his glasses asks.

"I'm his sister. That's just a boy from his school."

"OK, well, we will need to contact everyone's parents."

"I'm eighteen," Maisie says quickly.

The doctor smiles. "Yes, we will still need to contact Marco's parents, unless you are his guardian?"

She shakes her head and I see her eyes fill with tears. I don't really know what's happening but I can tell that she's scared. I look at Marco and he looks back at me with sad eyes.

"And you, young man, should be at school," the doctor says to me. "Can you ring your parents and get them to pick you up? We will need to have a quick chat with them too."

My face gets hot and I nod. The doctor leaves the room and I think I could probably run away right now. I could maybe find my way back to school and they wouldn't know any different. Marco and Maisie wouldn't tell on me, I'm pretty sure of that.

Just as I'm about to duck out of the curtain I bump into a lady coming the other way. She has a scarf on and smiles, as she stops me from falling.

"OK, buddy, where are you going in such a rush? We all need to have a chat before you go anywhere. I need to find out what's been going on."

I wonder if she's a police officer, but she doesn't have a badge or a uniform. She looks over at Marco and smiles.

"I will talk to you a bit later, sweetie, when you are feeling better." Then she turns to Maisie.

"Hello, Maisie," she says, and Maisie all of a sudden looks like a little girl. I don't know how they know each other but the lady opens the curtain and gestures to the chairs in the corridor. "Shall we have a catch-up, Maisie? It looks like Marco may need a bit more support, eh?"

They go through the curtain and the lady looks back at me. "Wait here with Marco. I will come and have a chat with you in a minute and we can get in touch with school and home and let them know where you are."

When she's gone, I look at Marco who looks a bit less pale, but whose face now looks tired and so sad.

"Who is that?" I ask. He pulls his mask away from his face.

"Social worker," he says. "We've been trying to avoid her."

"Why?" I ask. "She seems nice. Maybe she can help."

"Maisie thinks she won't let me live with her. She thinks she'll take me away and make me live with strangers."

Then he starts wheezing again and puts his mask back on. I feel suddenly panicky. I don't want to be here. I can't think in this airless room. I need to plan what on earth to do next. I feel the panic rising and I need to get out of this room. I need to breathe in some air. Marco can see that I'm struggling. He pulls off his mask again.

"Say you are going to the loo," he says. "Then get out of here."

"I hope you are OK," I say.

"Thanks for coming over," he says. "I know Maisie is cross but I'm glad you made her call the ambulance. You made the right choice."

Tears fill my eyes and I wipe them away quickly. It feels good to know that someone thinks I did the right thing.

I pass Maisie and the lady in the corridor and they don't even notice me. Once I'm out of the door I see the lift. I press the button and duck in.

Outside the hospital, I take a huge breath in. I can smell the sea and feel the sun on my face.

I go and sit on the beach and feel its instant calm wash over me. The scale of the sea and the sand making me feel safe and small. I breathe in the air and try and think about my options. All I know is that I have to stop lying. I don't know how to undo all the things that I've done. If I tell Madeleine and John, they will be so cross and disappointed. If I go back to Browtree, they will ask too many questions about where I have been. It's over. My adventure is over. Do I need to just come clean?

My tummy rumbles loudly and I open my bag to see if I have any more stolen snacks. I see the fabric of the Gains blazer, the stiff emblem staring up at me. Maybe this is the answer. Maybe it's a sign. Is there anything that I've done that can't be undone? Can I just go back and pretend that none of this ever happened? I stand up and take off my Browtree jumper. One more night of lying and then tomorrow morning maybe I can fix this mess.

At the bus stop the next morning my heart is racing. I can't believe I'm going to try and get away with this. Last night I snuck into John's office and sent an email from his account. My last lie. I told the Gains School that I had been unwell and would be starting there tomorrow. Browtree only have the wrong number for me anyway and so they won't be able to find me. Maybe I will never be found out.

When both buses turn up, I stare up at the Browtree bus and sigh. My Gains blazer feels big and itchy. When the doors to the Gains bus open and the driver looks at me, I stare back at him but my feet don't move.

"Are you getting on kid or what? Make a decision."

"Yes," I say. "Yes, I am." And I step on to the bus.

To find out what happens next, turn to **page 327**.

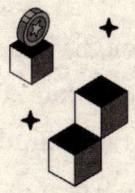

TELLING MARCO'S SECRET

"It was just some kid at the bus stop," I mumble. "He doesn't even go to the Gains."

"What did he say, Fred? It has clearly worried you."

I wonder if this is the right choice. Maybe I'm doing the wrong thing. I look at Madeleine's face and try to imagine her leaving me on my own for days. I give a little shake of my head. That would clearly never ever happen; she would be too worried about the mess I would make. And it makes me think, although Madeleine and John would never leave me or neglect me like that, it's not like I feel massively protected by them. It's weird that such opposites can still leave a kid feeling lonely. Maybe there is no perfect way to look after someone. Maybe all kids feel a bit alone.

There is a line, though, I guess, that just can't be crossed. You can't leave a kid in a house on his own. The way Madeleine and John don't understand me and choose not to see who I am is not ideal but it's not something to call social services about, is it? At least she's here now, listening. She really does care. It's just she has a funny way of showing it sometimes. A thought pops into my head, and before I can tell her anything about Marco, I need to do something else.

"Madeleine?" I ask.

"Yes."

"I think I might feel a tiny bit happier if I could call you Mum."

She looks completely shocked and her cheeks go a bit pink.

"I thought we were talking about a boy at the bus stop, Fred?"

"I know, but it made me think and I feel like I would prefer it. I know what you and John think about it, but that's how I feel. I just want to tell you the truth."

She looks flustered.

"Well, let me talk to John."

"Even if he doesn't want me to call him Dad, I could still call you Mum."

She softens a bit and sighs.

"Yes, maybe. Now, tell me about this boy. Do you know his name?"

I nod and then I tell her my version of the truth. I tell her his name and that he goes to Browtree and that his parents leave him home alone. I tell her that I just overheard the whole thing and that I have never met him or had anything to do with him.

When I'm finished, she leans in and gives me a squeeze.

"You have done the right thing, Fred. You can forget all about it now and get on with life at the Gains. We are very proud of you."

I smile, though I feel guilty that I haven't told her the whole truth about the Gains. When she gets to the door she turns and smiles.

"I don't think I would mind too much being called Mum, you know."

When the door closes, I flop back on to the bed and rub my face with my hands. I feel so confused. Telling the truth felt good. I felt closer to Madeleine, Mum, than I have in a long time. It felt good telling her what I thought. She said she was proud of me. But what will happen to Marco now?

The next day, I have freshened up my smelly

jumper and am heading into class. The chair-dancing Jared is messing about with some matches and the girls are all squealing at him. Marco's chair is empty and as I look towards the door to see if he is coming, a piece of lit paper lands by my foot and I stamp it out and the chair dancer scowls at me. If I had not been there to stamp it out the paper could have easily started a fire. I wonder what would have happened if I had sat next to the chair dancer.

When Marco is still not here for the register, I start to panic. What have I done? Have they taken him away or has he run away with Maisie? I didn't mention her to Madeleine.

At break I can't cope any more and I go to reception and ask where he is.

"He won't be in school today," the lady at the desk says.

Clearly she is not going to say anything else, even though I can tell that she knows something.

I run to the toilets and take out my phone:

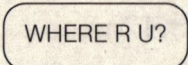

I wait for the whole of break time, staring at my screen, waiting to see that he has read it, but when the bell goes he's still not seen it. I call and it goes straight to voicemail. I try to picture what happened. Who did Madeleine call? What did they do?

This was a terrible idea. There is no way I can carry on for the whole day like this. Not knowing. Marco is in big trouble and all I tried to do was lie to save myself. I was so worried about not being found out I didn't think about what would actually happen next. About what would happen to Marco when the police or social workers or whoever went round.

I think about how it felt to talk to Madeleine. It felt good telling her the truth. Talking to her had been easier than I ever thought it would be. Maybe that's the only way out of this mess. When Marco finds out it was me who told then this will all be over anyway. He will tell school as soon as he can. My time at Browtree is over, whatever I do next. I need to know if he's OK and the only way to find out as soon as possible is to tell my secret too. Right now.

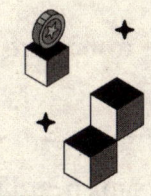

THE OFFICE

I leave the toilets and make my way down the hall. Kids are pushing past each other to get to their next lesson but I walk away from the classrooms and towards reception. The lady in the glasses looks up at me.

"You again. What can I do for you, Fred?"

I look at her and almost lose my nerve. I could make up something or even just ask about Marco again. Maybe she will tell me the truth this time. No, I know what I need to do.

"I need to call my mum," I say.

"Why is that, sweetie? Are you feeling poorly? I can send you to the nurse."

"No," I say, even though I do feel poorly. I feel like I might vomit at any minute.

"I'm not supposed to be here," I say. "I'm at the wrong school."

The lady twitches her head and looks over her glasses as though she's misheard me.

"What do you mean?"

"I'm meant to be at another school but I came here instead. That's why you didn't have my parents' details."

"But we called her. She left us a message."

"That wasn't her," I say.

I look at her with an apologetic smile and, as the truth sinks in, she is still for a while and then stands up so quickly that it makes me jump. She comes round the desk and takes my arm.

"Let's go and see Mrs Rumbelow."

As we walk into the office, Mrs Rumbelow's on the phone and the office lady writes something on a sheet of paper and puts it in front of Mrs Rumbelow, who immediately finishes her conversation and puts the phone down. She then looks up at us and waits for an explanation.

"Fred says he's supposed to be at another school but came here instead. He wants to call his mum."

Mrs Rumbelow looks confused and smiles at me.

"Do you want to tell me what's been going on, Fred?"

"I need to talk to Madeleine," I say. "I need to tell her everything and then I need to find out what happened to Marco."

"Is Madeleine your mum?"

The words start pouring out. Overlapping thoughts and tumbling truths fall out of my mouth.

"Yes, I told Madeleine – sorry, Mum – she says I can call her Mum now, maybe. Anyway, I told her all about Marco being on his own but I didn't tell her that I wasn't at the Gains and so she doesn't know I'm here but Marco is not here today and I'm terrified I made the wrong decision and that I should have kept his secret. So now I've got to tell my secret so that I can find out if he is OK."

The words keep pouring out of me, and even though I can see the confused look on Mrs Rumbelow's face I keep going.

"I need to call her but I gave you the wrong number so she wouldn't find out, but now she needs to find out, so can I call her?"

"Of course you can call her," Mrs Rumbelow says. "Can I ask one question, Fred, before you do, as this is all very difficult to understand?"

I nod, taking my phone out.

"Why did you come to Browtree?"

"Because I found the jumper at the bus stop, which felt like a sign, and I was fed up of being told what to do and who to be. I wanted to make a decision for myself for a change."

I pause and look at her face. I know that I'm making no sense and so I add, "I wanted to use the art room. I want to be an artist." When I say this I feel the tears prickle at the corners of my eyes. I try and blink them away and carry on but now my voice sounds different, like there's a ball of cotton wool in my throat.

"I don't want to be an athlete or any of the other things my parents think I should be. I just want to draw and paint and make things. I want to make a mess and see what happens. I want to let all the pictures and ideas in my brain out and I thought Browtree would be the best place to let that happen. But I was wrong, because now Marco is in trouble and it's all my fault."

The tears form fully now and as they fall down my cheeks and my nose starts running, Mrs Rumbelow hands me some tissues.

"Listen, Fred, it sounds like there is a lot going on for you. If you give me your mum's phone number, I can call her while you calm down a bit, and we can sort all this out. Everything is going to be OK."

"What about Marco? I told his secret and he might have run away or be hurt or something," I sniff.

"Marco is being looked after. Whatever you told your mum worked and someone went to check in on Marco and has taken him to be cared for. His asthma was quite bad, so they are making sure he is healthy and then he will be back at school in no time. It sounds to me, Fred, that you made exactly the right choice. Marco was not well and needed some help. You made sure he got it."

My breathing starts to slow and I wipe my eyes.

"I made the right choice? Really?" I ask.

"Yes." She nods kindly. "There are some secrets that are not OK to keep. Especially ones where someone is in danger. You did the right thing, Fred. Now, shall we do the right thing again and talk to your mum? It sounds like you need to start telling her some of the things you told us."

I nod and pass her my phone with Madeleine's number up on the screen.

"Hello, is this Fred's mum?" she says. "This is Mrs Rumbelow from Browtree High. There is nothing to worry about, Fred is with me. He is safe and well but he does have something that he needs to talk to you about."

I can hear my mum's voice on the other end of the phone. It sounds loud.

"Yes, he is here at Browtree. It seems that he decided to make some of his own schooling choices but has come to us and told us the truth now and would like to talk to you. He has been very brave and is a bit worried about telling you. I will put him on now."

She hands over the phone, and when I hold it to my ear I hear her voice.

"Fred, are you there? Fred?" She sounds scared.

"Hi, Mum," I say, and I hear her cry. "I'm OK but I did something silly. I think you should come and get me so we can talk about it."

"What about your father? I can call him and he can come from work. What on earth has been going on, Fred?"

"I will tell you when you come. Can I talk to you first and then we can tell John together later? I liked talking to you last night so I think it will be easier if it's just you."

There's a pause. She's thinking about what to do. Then I hear a little sigh and she blows her nose.

"Fine. I will be there in fifteen minutes."

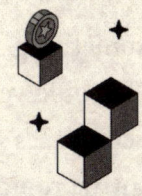

OWNING UP

When Mum arrives, Mrs Rumbelow has a chat with her and then she leaves us to talk in the office. She has put out tissues and biscuits and Mum takes a tissue and blows her nose. She has clearly been crying the whole way here.

"What has been going on, Fred? You've been lying to us."

I nod.

"Why would you do this?" She blows her nose again. "I mean, I've been racking my brains thinking of reasons, but I just don't understand. We decided that the Gains was the best school, so why would you come here? I remember you saying that you liked it here but we decided. We all decided together."

"No, we didn't," I say. "John decided, like he always

does. I tried to say something. I tried to ask you, but you didn't listen. I should've tried harder. I was scared of the Gains School. It's huge and terrifying and I didn't even see an art room there."

"Honestly, Fred, this can't all be over some silly pictures. You can doodle anywhere, surely?"

Then I feel a rush of clarity and anger. I look at her.

"It's not doodling," I say, more loudly than I mean to. "They are not silly pictures. It's the thing I love most and you cannot ignore it or squash it any more. It's who I am and it feels like you are ignoring me and squashing me. I know that you don't get it, that you see it as mess and clutter, but can't you understand it's important to me? So important that I got on the wrong bus."

She shakes her head and puts her hands to her face, as though she is trying not to listen.

"If you carry on ignoring it then this will keep happening, Mum. I will have to lie and hide things from you. I've been hiding my paintings from you for ages. They are taped up behind the boring boat pictures in my room."

"Really?" she says. "No. I would have seen them when I clean."

"Nope, they are there. I'll show you, if you promise

not to throw them away or call them doodles or silliness." I pause and she looks at me, her face getting redder. I'm not sure if I should carry on, or if I've gone too far. When she reaches her hand out, I hold mine out and she grabs on tightly. I feel like telling the truth is the right thing to do.

"Last night I told you about Marco and it felt right. It felt good telling you the truth, so now I'm telling you the truth about me."

"What about John?" she whispers, almost to herself. "He will be furious."

"I know. He wants me to be just like him, but I'm not. If I have you on my side, though, maybe he will start to understand?"

She takes a biscuit as we sit in silence for a while, both thinking about what will happen next. After a few minutes she stands up.

"Right, well, let's go home, shall we?"

"What do you think he will do?" I ask.

"He will try and make you go to the Gains School, that's for sure," she says.

I nod and let out a huge sigh. Then she adds, "But let's see what happens, eh? Well done for telling the truth, Fred. About Marco and now about you. I promise I have listened. I will do my best."

As we get in the car, she closes the door and puts her seat belt on.

"I was reorganizing under the stairs this morning and wondering what to do with it. Maybe it could make a good mini art studio?"

I smile and feel more tears form in my eyes. Different tears this time, though. Tears of relief and happiness.

"Thanks, Mum," I say. I lean over and give her a big hug.

"It had better be the tidiest art studio the world has ever seen, Fred, that's all I'm saying!"

When we pull up to the house I turn to her.

"Can I go for a quick walk? I need to clear my head before I talk to John." I need the sound of the waves and the size of the sea in the distance to calm my buzzing brain. Whatever happens next will be OK if I have been to the beach.

She purses her lips.

"Honestly, Fred, you don't half push it." But then she shakes her head. "Fine. Ten minutes, OK?"

I give her another hug and turn and walk towards the sea.

To find out what happens next, turn to **page 323**.

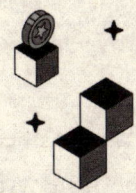

ONE MONTH LATER (STORY ENDING 1)

"I was a complete idiot. I'm sorry."

My heart's thumping in my chest. I hear Rupert on the other end of the phone breathing out and I can't tell what he is feeling, so I carry on.

"You would have made a great friend and I wasn't thinking straight. I have trouble making decisions and knowing what to do, but I know I made a terrible choice not sticking with you. I'm sorry."

"Are your parents making you say this?" he asks quietly.

"No! They make me do a lot of stuff but talking about my feelings is definitely not one of them."

"Everyone at school was talking about it for ages.

Why did Mrs Ketsgrove leave? What did she say to you?"

"I guess she's the reason I'm calling. She made me realize that if I do something wrong I should try and make up for it. Be the person I really want to be."

"And you want to be my friend?"

"Yeah," I whisper, trying to sound normal even though my throat is feeling tight. There's a big pause as though he is thinking. My tummy feels fluttery and sick, as the guilt of everything I did floods through me again.

"What school are you at now?" Rupert asks.

"John got me into this other strict school. It's just like the Gains but miles away. They do have a great art department, though."

"Ah, that's cool. And thanks for the picture, by the way. I really liked it."

I dropped the picture off a couple of weeks ago but didn't have the courage to knock on the door. I chickened out and ran away. Today's the first day I felt like I could do it. I'm not sure why saying sorry can be so hard.

"How's robotics?" I ask.

"Awesome."

We chat about school and family and when we

hang up, I feel a bit lighter. I'm not sure if he has forgiven me but it feels good to have said sorry, and you never know, maybe if I show him that I can be a good friend he might forgive me in time.

With my bum wedged and wiggled into the sand I stare out and listen to the waves. Every breath in feels bigger than the last.

I think back to the day at the bus stop. The panicky feeling, not knowing what to do. I used to feel like that about almost everything. Whether I should have an apple or an orange. What TV show to watch. Which thought to think. Choices would terrify me. It felt like any tiny decision could ruin my life, but I don't feel like that now. Maybe making these huge choices and getting things wrong along the way is OK. Maybe I have to get things wrong so I can see the right way too.

I guess it's not always about the choices I make but what I do next that matters. If I had to do it all again, I don't know what I would have done differently.

What would you do differently? Turn back to **page 22** to make some different choices.

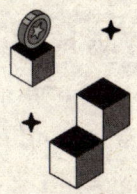

ONE MONTH LATER (STORY ENDING 2)

So much has happened in the last month. I have apologized, cried, laughed and talked more than I have ever talked before. I know now that whatever decision I make, it's not the end of the world if it's the wrong one. It turns out I'm not that bad at talking, at putting stuff right.

When I got back from Rupert's I was grounded and not allowed anywhere for three weeks. It was so hard not being able to come here, to the beach. Mr Sourden let me come back to school and I had detention every lunchtime for a week – with Callum. So that was not fun. He's left me and Rupert alone though ever since. I'm even thinking of going back to basketball club, but Rupert says there is no way he's setting foot on that court ever again. He says he will just cheer from the side. Jessie has made some pom-poms.

Even though Madeleine and John were angry with me for walking off, they kind of listened. I think they knew something had changed. Something inside me. There are still rules obviously … and they are still Madeleine and John; Mum and Dad was "a step too far", apparently! But I was allowed to join art club and Madeleine even bought a washable tablecloth for me to paint on at home. I'm only allowed to do it once a week and she gets so anxious and fretful about the carpet that I can't really relax but she's trying. I think John was weirdly impressed with me starting a fight. He asked if I wanted to join a wrestling team. I said no, obviously, I can't think of anything worse. But I know what he means. He's proud of me for standing up for myself, and so am I. I just need to do it everywhere, at home with them, at school and inside myself. If I do it all the time – with words – then there will be no reason to fight.

He's really trying, I can tell. The other day he asked me who my favourite artist was. He didn't know what to say when I said M.C. Escher. His face looked so confused it made me laugh. It was like in French lessons when you ask a question but have no idea what to say when someone actually answers you. That must be what it's like for him now with me, like learning a new language. I showed him pictures on my phone of my favourites and he got it, or he tried to at least. It felt nice.

With my bum wedged and wiggled into the sand I stare out and listen to the waves. Every breath in feels bigger than the last. I think back to the day at the bus stop. The panicky feeling, not knowing what to do. I used to feel like that about almost everything. Whether I should have an apple or an orange. What TV show to watch. Which thought to think. Choices would terrify me. It felt like any tiny decision could ruin my life but I don't feel like that now. Maybe making these huge choices and getting things wrong along the way is OK. Maybe it's more than OK. Maybe I have to get things wrong so I can see the right way too.

I guess it's not always about the choices I make but what I do next that matters. If I had to do it all again, I don't know what I would have done differently.

What would you do differently? Turn back to **page 22** to make some different choices.

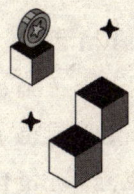

ONE MONTH LATER (STORY ENDING 3)

Even though I moved to Browtree, I ride a bike with Rupert most days after school and I go round for tea every Thursday. Last week Jessie, his sister, made these fancy potatoes with a funny name – dolphin waz. Sounds like dolphin wee but they were delicious. He's at the dentist tonight so I'm at the beach on my own. Browtree is pretty cool. I've not really made any great mates so far. I sit next to a kid called Marco who constantly has a Rubik's cube in his hand. He's OK, but I think he has a lot going on; he's off school a lot. Most of the time I'm in the art room. It's just as good as I remember it and I have done some really cool paintings.

John was quiet and angry for quite a long time after everything that happened at the Gains. I would hear Madeleine whispering to him at night telling him that everything was going to be OK and to look at how happy I am. How it's all worth it. Whatever she said must have worked in the end. He is still quiet but the anger has gone. The other day when I was putting my dishes in the dishwasher, he patted me on the back and said he was proud of me. I nearly dropped my plate!

Madeleine seems brighter somehow – lighter. I think it's the first time she has really stuck up for me. Maybe for herself. She's quite into my art. I bring it home for her to see. She still won't let me paint at home but she says that as I have the art room at Browtree there is no need to mess up her house.

With my bum wedged and wiggled into the sand I stare out and listen to the waves. Every breath in feels bigger than the last. I think back to the day at the bus stop. The panicky feeling, not knowing what to do. I used to feel like that about almost everything. Whether I should have an apple or an orange. What TV show to watch. Which thought to think. Choices would terrify me. It felt like any tiny decision could ruin my life but I don't feel like that now. Maybe making these huge choices and getting things wrong along the way is OK. Maybe it's more than OK. Maybe I have to get things wrong so I can see the right way too.

I guess it's not always about the choices I make but what I do next that matters. If I had to do it all again, I don't know what I would have done differently.

> What would you do differently? Turn back to **page 22** to make some different choices.

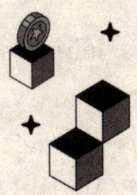

ONE MONTH LATER
(STORY ENDING 4)

Our bikes are on the sand and Rupert is looking for crabs in the rock pools. It's nice having a best friend.

I was in detention every day for three weeks and painting the toilets took for ever. Some massive Year Seven kid took a picture of the graffiti before I had painted over it and turned it into a poster. He put it up all over the school and in everyone's lockers and when everyone found out it was me, I became a bit of a celebrity. People were asking me to draw pictures on their books and their bags and sign things. It was pretty cool actually.

Miss Nolan the art teacher found us another room for art club and I go and paint every lunchtime, apart from on robotics days. John is still grumpy that I'm not on a sports team, but I'm trying to be more honest with them, like Rupert tells me to be, and it seems to be working a bit. They are still the same people. It's still the same meals at the same time and the house is still immaculate, but slowly I'm starting to feel a bit more like myself and not just a version of what they want me to be.

With my bum wedged and wiggled into the sand I stare out and listen to the waves. Every breath in feels bigger than the last. I think back to the day at the bus stop. The panicky feeling, not knowing what to do. I used to feel like that about almost everything. Whether I should have an apple or an orange. What TV show to watch. Which thought to think. Choices would terrify me. It felt like any tiny decision could ruin my life but I don't feel like that now. Maybe making these huge choices and getting things wrong along the way is OK. Maybe it's more than OK. Maybe I have to get things wrong so I can see the right way too.

I guess it's not always about the choices I make but what I do next that matters. If I had to do it all again, I don't know what I would have done differently.

What would you do differently? Turn back to **page 22** to make some different choices.

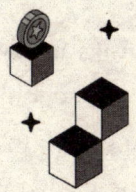

ONE MONTH LATER (STORY ENDING 5)

John was furious, which was no surprise. But Mum said to leave it to her and she told him everything. I don't think I have ever seen her so calm before. It was like she was taking control for the first time in her life and not by cleaning or fretting, but by saying exactly what she thought. I could hear her from my spot at the top of the stairs.

"I think if he wanted to go to that school so badly then we need to listen to him and understand his reasons. Maybe he has a point, John? We can't control him for ever. He is growing up. He helped that poor boy and clearly the teachers there all think he's pretty marvellous. Maybe that's where he belongs."

They argued about it for days and I had a whole week of not going to any school at all. John shouted and talked about being a Gains boy, but she didn't back down. I don't know what made her so sure. So confident about sticking up for me. I think it might have been the night I decided to tell her the truth. That might have been the decision that changed things. Or maybe it was a different decision, one that I didn't even really know I was making.

Eventually John realized that she would battle about this for ever and he gave in. I couldn't believe it. Now I have a jumper that doesn't smell of mushrooms and I go to the art room every day. Marco came back to school and he doesn't speak to me any more. He looks sad and I do feel really bad. Apparently he had to go and live with a different family, so I guess that means he won't get to run away with Maisie. Mum says that telling her was still the right thing to do even if he can't see it.

With my bum wedged and wiggled into the sand I stare out and listen to the waves. Every breath in feels bigger than the last. I think back to the day at the bus stop. The panicky feeling, not knowing what to do. I used to feel like that about almost everything. Whether I should have an apple or an orange.

What TV show to watch. Which thought to think. Choices would terrify me. It felt like any tiny decision could ruin my life, but I don't feel like that now. Maybe making these huge choices and getting things wrong along the way is OK. Maybe it's more than OK. Maybe I have to get things wrong so I can see the right way too.

I guess it's not always about the choices I make but what I do next that matters. If I had to do it all again, I don't know what I would have done differently.

> What would you do differently? Turn back to **page 22** to make some different choices.

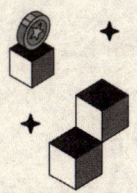

ONE MONTH LATER (STORY ENDING 6)

Everything went pretty smoothly the day I turned up to the Gains. I was put in a class and no one really seemed to notice that I had been missing. They sat me next to some scary kid called Callum, who is pretty mean. He's not as scary as the Gains School itself, though, with its big corridors and angry-looking teachers.

When I got home that first day Madeleine had a confused look on her face.

"I had a voicemail today, Fred, from the head teacher at Browtree. She was back at school after her operation and seemed very confused. She seemed to think you were going to Browtree. She was asking where you were. I've only just heard the message.

I can't imagine what on earth she is talking about."

By that point I must have become so devious, the lies just fell out of my mouth.

"Oh, maybe she just got confused. She has been in hospital, hasn't she? Maybe she's on some really strong painkillers."

I pulled a funny face and crossed my eyes and realized I might have been overdoing it when Madeleine looked at me suspiciously. Then she saw the dinner was burning and started flapping about.

"Just call and leave her a message telling them I'm a Gains boy." Then as the panic of being caught set in I added, "Do it now, so you don't forget. Better on the voicemail … especially if she is full of painkillers."

That was the only time I even got close to being found out. I almost wanted to tell her, so that I could let it all out. I thought it was the best choice, keeping it all a secret and just going to the Gains, but the lies and the secrets about what I've done and who I am have felt so heavy. I thought I was winning by getting away with it, but that's not really how it feels now.

Hiding away at school, trying not to be noticed. Every teatime, smiling and pretending that everything is fine. I've felt myself getting smaller and smaller. I've even stopped drawing. It's time to tell them. I know it is. I want to go back and put it all right. Make decisions that feel right and tell the truth.

With my bum wedged and wiggled into the sand I stare out and listen to the waves. Every breath in feels bigger than the last. I think back to the first day at the bus stop. The panicky feeling, not knowing what to do. I used to feel like that about almost everything. Whether I should have an apple or an orange. What TV show to watch. Which thought to think. Choices would terrify me. It felt like any tiny decision could ruin my life but I don't feel like that now. Maybe making these huge choices and getting things wrong along the way is OK. Maybe it's more than OK. Maybe I have to get things wrong so I can see the right way too.

I guess it's not always about the choices I make but what I do next that matters. If I had to do it all again, I don't know what I would have done differently.

What would you do differently? Turn back to **page 22** to make some different choices.

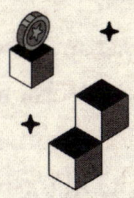

ONE MONTH LATER (STORY ENDING 7)

There have been a lot of decisions to make since I left Browtree and started at the Gains. I have been really trying to listen for the voice to show me the right way. I think it's working. I have just about avoided the bullies so far and my new friend Rupert is helping me to figure out how to tell my parents that the football and rugby teams really aren't for me. The other day I came home with a nosebleed and ripped shorts – it's brutal.

He thinks it's time to tell them that I want to be an artist and show them all my drawings. We have made a plan that I'm going to leave out one of my pictures and see what Madeleine says. I know he's right. I need to be honest.

Whatever happens from now, I know that I'll be fine. Even if I made bad decisions, and knowing that I will make bad decisions again in the future, I think that I'll get through it. Right now in this moment I think I could get through anything. I will find a way to speak out or tell the truth or make up for things I do wrong. I will be kind and try and make the right choices, and I will say sorry when I don't.

With my bum wedged and wiggled into the sand I stare out and listen to the waves. Every breath in feels bigger than the last. I think back to the day at the bus stop. The panicky feeling, not knowing what to do. I used to feel like that about almost everything. Whether I should have an apple or an orange. What TV show to watch. Which thought to think. Choices would terrify me. It felt like any tiny decision could ruin my life, but I don't feel like that now. Maybe making these huge choices and getting things wrong along the way is OK. Maybe it's more than OK. Maybe I have to get things wrong so I can see the right way too.

I guess it's not always about the choices I make but what I do next that matters. If I had to do it all again, I don't know what I would have done differently.

What would you do differently? Turn back to **page 22** to make some different choices.

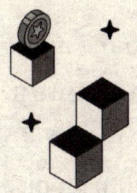

ONE MONTH LATER (STORY ENDING 8)

John begged and pleaded, and eventually the Gains gave me a chance. I am on probation and if I do even the tiniest thing wrong, I will be out and have to go who knows where. So I am grounded and stuck in a school that doesn't really want me.

The Gains turned out to be as terrifying as I thought, but to be honest, as it's currently the only place I'm allowed to go to, it's better than being stuck in my bedroom. I've even made a friend. He's called Rupert and as soon as I'm allowed out again I'm going to go round to his house for tea. His little sister wants to go on *Junior MasterChef*, apparently, so she is trying out dishes. I can't wait to see his house.

He has described it to me and I feel like I've already been there. Like I can picture it.

I did go back to Browtree. To apologize to Marco. It was awkward. He didn't look at me and just clicked away at his Rubik's cube. It didn't make me feel much better, to be honest, but then maybe sometimes we don't deserve to feel any better.

The other day on the way back from school I think I spotted Jared coming out of an empty house. He looked exactly the same. I wonder if he will ever think about making different decisions.

Today I was allowed to get on the school bus instead of being picked up. As soon as I got off, I ran as fast as I could to the beach; it's the only place I want to be. I have missed it so much. Just a few minutes before I dust off the sand and head back to my bedroom prison.

With my bum wedged and wiggled into the sand I stare out and listen to the waves. Every breath in feels bigger than the last. I think back to the day at the bus stop. The panicky feeling, not knowing what to do. I used to feel like that about almost everything. Whether I should have an apple or an orange. What TV show to watch. Which thought to think. Choices would terrify me. It felt like any tiny decision could ruin my life but I don't feel like that now. Maybe making these huge choices and getting things wrong along the way is OK. Maybe it's more than OK. I guess we have to get things wrong so we can see the right way too.

I guess it's not always about the choices I make but what I do next that matters. If I had to do it all again, I don't know what I would have done differently.

> What would you do differently? Turn back to **page 22** to make some different choices.

THE DECISION MAP
Have you followed all the paths?

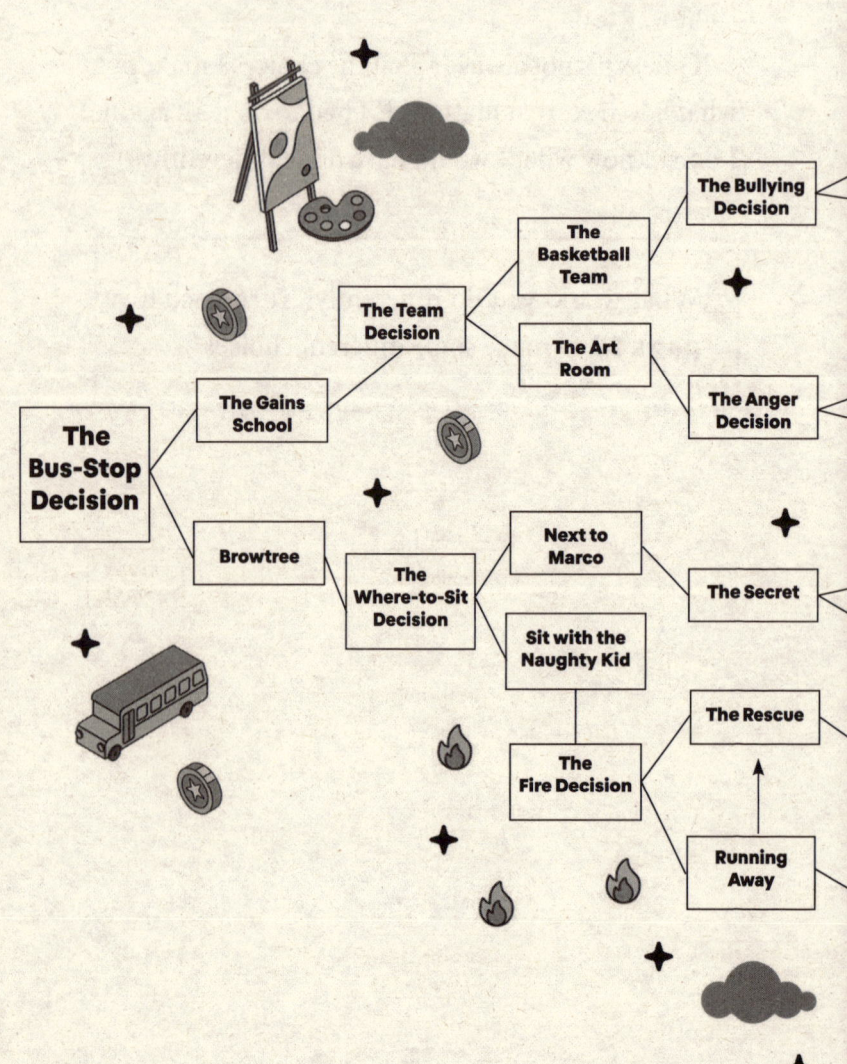

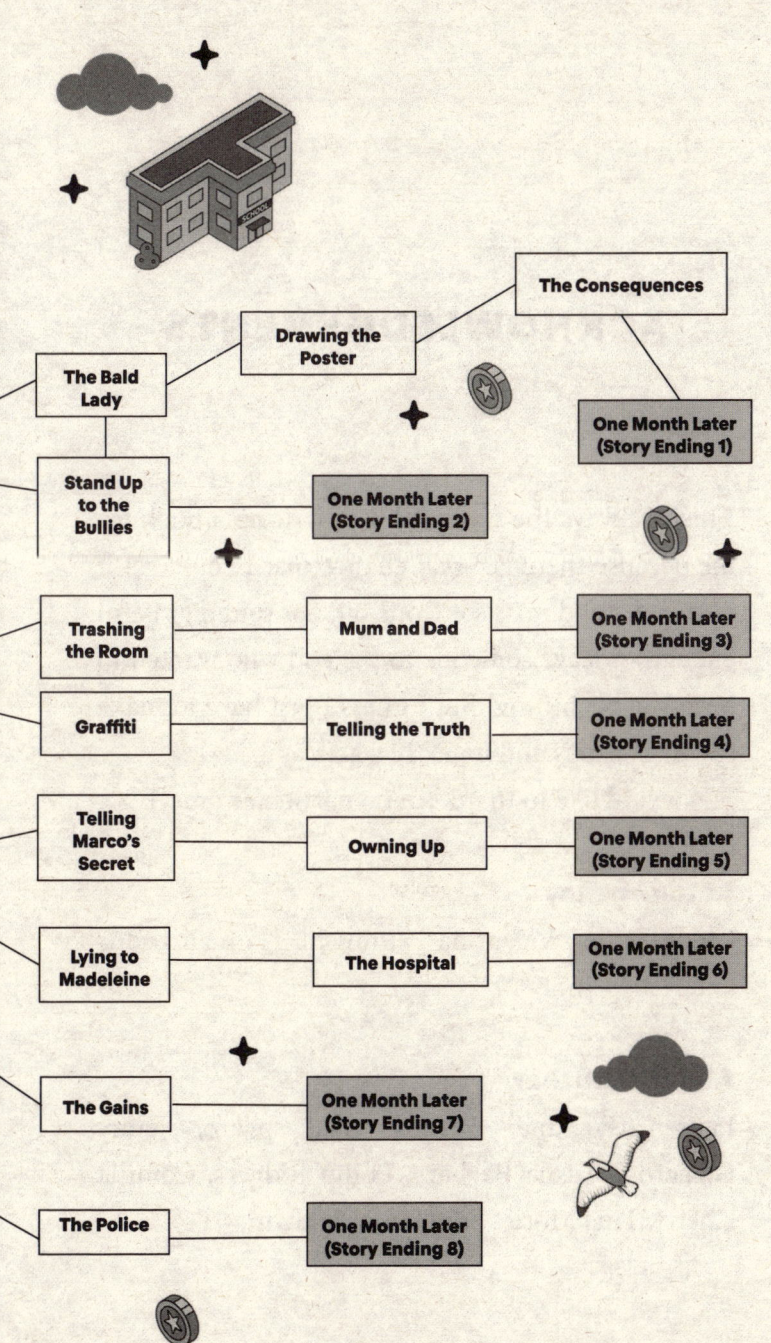

ACKNOWLEDGEMENTS

This is always the hardest bit of writing a book for me because there is a real chance that I could get it wrong. I could miss someone off, not sound grateful enough or leave someone to the end who wanted to be at the beginning! But I guess I just have to make some decisions and hope they are right.

I would like to thank (in no particular order):

At the agency
Chloe Seager, Valentina Paulmichl, Hannah Ladds and Kelly Chin.

At the publisher
Lauren Fortune, Wendy Shakespeare, Jenny Glencross, Susila Baybars, Philip Ridgers, Camilla Chetty, Tina Mories and Sarah Baldwin.

At my house
Rob Rouse, Lenny, Cleo, G. Bean, Billy Whizz

In my life
Gaz and Jools, Imogen and Nara, Cat and Ru, Colette, Kate, Zoe, Rosie and all at the Deli, Book Club, Art Club, FFF, the comics, the writers, the family and friends old and new.

In the book world
The wonderful teachers, librarians, booksellers, reviewers, parents and readers.

You have all helped me to keep making the decision to write, so thank you all.